Who Were the
Real Oliver Twists?

Who Were the Real Oliver Twists?

Childhood Poverty in Victorian London

Lynn Hamilton

PEN & SWORD HISTORY

First published in Great Britain in 2024 by
Pen & Sword History
An imprint of Pen & Sword Books Limited
Yorkshire – Philadelphia

ISBN 978 1 39905 454 6

Typeset by Mac Style
Printed in the UK by CPI Group (UK) Ltd, Croydon, CR0 4YY.

Pen & Sword Books Limited incorporates the imprints of After
the Battle, Atlas, Archaeology, Aviation, Discovery, Family History,
Fiction, History, Maritime, Military, Military Classics, Politics,
Select, Transport, True Crime, Air World, Frontline Publishing, Leo
Cooper, Remember When, Seaforth Publishing, The Praetorian Press,
Wharncliffe Local History, Wharncliffe Transport, Wharncliffe True
Crime and White Owl.

For a complete list of Pen & Sword titles please contact

PEN & SWORD BOOKS LIMITED
47 Church Street, Barnsley, South Yorkshire, S70 2AS, England
E-mail: enquiries@pen-and-sword.co.uk
Website: www.pen-and-sword.co.uk
or
PEN AND SWORD BOOKS
1950 Lawrence Rd, Havertown, PA 19083, USA
E-mail: uspen-and-sword@casematepublishers.com
Website: www.penandswordbooks.com

Contents

Acknowledgements

Though he needs no acknowledgement, Charles Dickens inspires this book. Through his characters, he explored every kind of human desperation without leaving us, his rapt readers, hopeless. I would also like to acknowledge the indefatigable Henry Mayhew and John Pounds, reformers who did not fear contamination by the poor in an age when class segregation was perhaps the strongest it ever was. More recent scholars – Jeannie Duckworth, Louise Raw, and Viviana Zelizer – also lit the way through the painful labyrinth of child labour, trafficking, and unjust punishments.

This book is dedicated to my husband, Joel Parker Worth III, who made me strong enough to chase my dreams.

Introduction: The Worst Poor Law Ever

The most poignant image in Charles Dickens's nineteenth-century novel, *Oliver Twist*, is that of a small orphan boy with a bowl in his hand. His bowl is empty, but he is still hungry. His clothes are rags. His face is a petition. Behind and all around him are other starving, desperate boys. Standing before him is an evil man – tyrannical and violent. The boy summons all the courage he has and says, 'Please, sir, I want some more.'

When we actually read Charles Dickens's *Oliver Twist*, we find that Oliver never volunteered to ask for seconds. He was certainly brave, but nowhere near hungry enough to challenge authority in a workhouse where thrashings were dealt out for much less than open rebellion against the system.

Twist's peer had just threatened to cannibalise him if he didn't get up there and demand seconds. Somehow, the film adaptations of *Oliver Twist* never quite capture the full horror of the original text. Possibly because film audiences could not handle the full-on darkness into which the novel frequently sinks.

Second helpings were specifically prohibited at the Cleveland Street Workhouse. And that was the workhouse on which Charles Dickens carefully modelled Oliver Twist's childhood prison. To understand why Oliver and his real-life counterparts were being systematically starved to death, we must first understand the Poor Law Amendment Act of 1834. The amendment was casually referred to as the 'new poor law'.

It should have been called the 'worst poor law ... ever'.

Britain's poor laws originated with the hard-working and no-nonsense Queen Elizabeth I. In 1598 and 1601, these new laws required parishes to feed their starving residents with taxes collected for that purpose. Today, we take such a safety net for granted, but, in their day, these brand-new laws completely changed the playing field. Previously, if crops failed or prices soared, it was accepted as inevitable that many people would quietly die of starvation or exposure. But someone in Elizabeth's cabinet had the extraordinary idea that people are not savages, and should not let others perish of want when it was possible to prevent such deaths.

Down the centuries, Britain's poor laws were frequently amended, often with unintended negative consequences. The system that prevailed prior to the new poor law was far from perfect and often led to casual cruelty, especially when local communities felt the pinch of having to provide for those who had nothing.

Under this system, children (some orphaned, some not), disabled old people, and those with severe mental illness were often housed together in parish houses. These houses were overseen by parish leaders, often appointed and serving grudgingly. To understand Victorian hostility toward the poor, it is important to note that the money to support the parish houses had to come from residents of the parish, in the form of a parish tax. Parishioners could be extremely resentful about the money squeezed from them to support what people routinely called 'paupers'.

The story of Robert Blinco, which comes up later in this book, illustrates the limitations and benefits of this system. Child residents of these parish houses were sent to work at a young age, often as young as 6, in order to lessen the burden of the poor on the parish. But, in the meantime, they were fed properly, clothed decently, and even provided with soap and water.

Under this loosely organised system of charity, parishes also provided gifts of money and food to impoverished adults and allowed them to stay in their homes, if they still had them. This system sustained local families that had short-term or seasonal poverty. For instance, in the winter, when home-grown food was scarce, farm families could apply for and receive enough to get them through the hard months. A mother of five, whose husband had fallen sick or lost his job, could also hope to provide food for her family while keeping a roof over their heads until they were back on their financial feet. Such charity was provided by wealthy families, churches, and local government. This kind of merciful welfare was called, very confusingly, 'outdoor relief'. The archetype of outdoor relief is a man or woman standing outside a church, handing out bread to whomever asks for it.

Hablot K. Brown, who illustrated many of Charles Dickens's books under the pseudonym name 'Phiz', provided a drawing titled 'Outdoor Relief' that perfectly captures its necessity and dangers. In this drawing, a fat man with an officious-looking staff, the symbol of leadership, stands outside a building at the top of the stairs. He is the dispenser of charity. A woman, perhaps a mother, is doling out food to at least seven small children. At least two of the figures in the foreground are severely disabled, one looks to be fatally malnourished and half naked.

But there are also at least two figures who look to be young, able-bodied adults. They appear to be fighting over the free food.

These two freeloaders haunted the Victorian consciousness, just as they haunt the consciousness of today's taxpayers. In any system for ensuring that welfare gets to those in genuine need, there will always be those who have learned to game that system. Most philanthropists and non-profit organisations graciously accept that a portion of any aid will go to bad operators. Better to benefit a few freeloaders than to let anyone go without the basic necessities is the underlying philosophy of most charities.

But the flip side to this mercy is the rage of taxpayers who believe that aid to the poor is direct theft from those who work hard and pay their way. Such thinking reasons that the poor are lazy, greedy, and of poor moral fibre. Victorians were many things. Reformers lived among them, but many wealthy and middle-class Victorians openly despised the poor, blaming them for their condition, and assuming that they must be lazy or dishonest or both. Even the children of poverty were treated with suspicion. Children who grew up in a workhouse and had, it could be argued, very limited opportunities to get into mischief, would not be hired as servants in good homes. The owners of those good homes reserved the right to discriminate based on 'origins'.

This naked hatred of the poor, the homeless, the orphans, the disabled, the elderly, the addicted, and the mentally ill underpinned the new poor law. The politicians who wrote it channelled the rage of their constituents. But on paper, they didn't admit to the raw hatred. Instead, they pointed to the philosophers, one in particular.

Preacher-Driven Policy

In the nineteenth and twentieth centuries, philosophers were frequently invoked as the justification for specific abominations that they did not intend. Thomas Robert Malthus was an Anglican minister and amateur economist whose ideas took on a sinister life of their own, in the hands of unscrupulous politicians. Malthus, it should be noted, was dead only a few short months after the new poor law received royal assent.

Malthus's great insight was that an expansion of resources would always be followed by an increase in population. This increased population would stress out the expanded resources, cancelling out the benefit of resource expansion. Malthus's take on charity to the poor was sorely fatalistic. When the poor got free food, they would recklessly make more babies and create an even greater drain on community resources, Malthus posited. He described what he saw as a vicious and unbreakable cycle in which the struggle to keep a growing population fed, watered, clothed, and housed was never ending. In his mind, population growth was the great evil, and the poor were a sad byproduct of that evil.

Why Malthus looms such a spectre in British public policy and Aldous Huxley's futuristic fable, *Brave New World*, remains a mystery to some. One imagines a college freshman writing, with enthusiastic belief in his own originality, that a runaway population will quickly run out of food and other amenities. One then imagines a weary professor penning a marginal comment along the lines of: 'Try making a claim that is not obvious to most educated people.'

Malthus recklessly advocated eliminating all public and private aid to the poor. He believed that withholding this aid would encourage people to marry later in life and limit the size of their families. He was trained in letters and the church, not in economics, and history has proven his theory only partly correct. He failed to predict the complex impacts that industrialisation would have on global economies – even though the industrial revolution was taking place right in front of him.

How much less, then, was this courageous cleric able to predict the outcomes that widely available birth control would have on the populations of advanced nation states? Nor was it in Malthus's gift to predict how the empowerment of women would influence his equation. One imagines him, somehow resurrected in the twenty-first century, reeling in wonder at the declining populations of Italy and Japan. In countries where women control their own money, land, real estate, and contraception, they do an *impressive* job of keeping their family size proportionate to their wealth in contravention of all that Malthus's depressive gloom portended.

Malthus's ideas could have been used as the springboard for a widespread education effort aimed at showing families why they should voluntarily limit the number of children they had. Public funds used to build workhouses and hire directors could have been used to increase and diversify food production.

Instead, Parliament interpreted Malthus in a way that was suspiciously aligned with their inclinations to blame the victims of poverty and discourage applications for public aid in the most inhumane ways imaginable.

Cruelties of the New Poor Law

One of the cruelties of the new poor law was the prohibition of most outdoor relief. Private charity was effectively outlawed. The new law focused attention on the 'able bodied'. If a man or woman were able to work, the law reasoned, he or she should work, even though many willing workers were unable to find work. Unwed mothers were effectively unemployable; displaced agricultural workers lacked transferable skills; factories were allowed to use free child labour instead of paying adults living wages. Where, under previous laws, families and individuals could be given food, blankets, shoes, coal, firewood, etc., under the new law, these acts of kindness were actually prohibited. The poor were not allowed to beg or even receive unsolicited gifts. They were, instead, obliged to go to the workhouse.

Under the new poor law, workhouses were redesigned and newly constructed because the old parish houses and poor houses simply were not vicious enough. The new workhouses were, effectively, prisons. The poor were the felons of these institutions; their punishment was hard labour and a diet so low in calories that they were constantly on the brink of starvation. Admission to a workhouse meant that one could have his head shaved and his clothes replaced with a uniform.

The intent is obvious. Workhouses were meant to be a deterrent. The underlying belief of the new poor law was that legislation could scare people out of poverty. And it was not just able-bodied adults that were expected to work for their food. Children, the elderly, and the disabled were expected to get out of bed and do an honest day's work to avoid the workhouse.

The cost of constructing the new workhouses would have fed quite a few people. This fact was not lost on northern English counties who argued against the forced construction of these institutions. Activists from the north believed that their previous system of charity worked better. Poverty in those counties was cyclical, not chronic, they noted. The poor, in other words, rallied when prices dropped or when their crops recovered. These costly workhouses would sit empty for most of the year, opponents argued.

The new workhouses were deliberately designed to break up and demoralise families. To that end, they were designed with four sections. Wives were shunted off to one wing, husbands to another, girl children to a third, and their brothers to the fourth. To enter such a place with your children was to take the risk of never seeing them – or your spouse – again. Any student of history can see why families frequently chose to starve together and live on the streets, or in swamps or forests, rather than enter the workhouse.

Under the new poor law, workhouses were run, not by men of God or medicine, but by businessmen. These leaders cared much more about saving money for their monied peers than they did about providing humanitarian aid. If a workhouse director did have a charitable bone or two in his body, the local merchants and wealthy landowners to whom he reported would remind him that his job was to save them money. These directors, with the help of a local committee, determined what kind of food the inmates would receive and how much. Stinginess became a science dedicated to discovering how little you could feed people without killing them.

The new poor law twisted the knife particularly hard on unwed mothers and their entirely guiltless offspring. Under the previous poor laws, parishes would investigate an illegitimate pregnancy and, where possible, force the father to pay child support. In many cases, local parish leaders even forced that libertine into marriage with the mother of his child. This insistence on paternal responsibility was, in fact, dictated by the Poor Law of 1733. Under that law, unwed mothers could, at least theoretically, have deadbeat fathers arrested and imprisoned if they failed in their duties of child support.

At the very lowest circle of new poor law hell was the freedom of a mother to abandon her own illegitimate child with no legal consequences. Here, in all its naked ugliness, was the Victorian contempt for children unmasked, with illegitimate children enjoying a status about equal to insects.

If an unwed mother chose to keep, and attempt to raise her child, the new poor law made that child her legal responsibility alone. No longer could a woman ask local authorities to require the father of her child to do any right thing. He could not be compelled to marry her; he could not even be compelled to pay a pittance for food, clothing, housing, or medical care. A local squire might be the known father of a local bastard, but that baby's poverty-stricken mother would bear the entire financial burden for her child's upbringing.

And bringing that child up would be particularly difficult for a woman wearing, effectively, the scarlet letter of unwed sex. Women known to have illegitimate children had terrible difficulty finding employment. Most wealthy households would not hire them as servants. Even factories might turn them away. Into the workhouses they went, therefore, with their babies and with very few chances of ever getting out alive.

Today, it might be difficult even for the most ardent Trumpist to understand the contempt with which Victorians treated illegitimate children. The contempt of men, themselves in no danger of having to support the unplanned child, can be chalked down to casual indifference. But even women poured vitriol on the victims of seduction and rape. Ann Caltman proved that when she beat up her 13-year-old servant so badly that local law enforcers became involved. Their investigation discovered that the beaten child was Caltman's own illegitimate daughter.[1]

Critics of the new poor law noted, with some insight, that this legal amendment made it easier for wealthy men to seduce young, vulnerable women, possibly even their own employees, and skate off with no consequences. The obvious inequity of that law led twenty-first century writer Susan Zlotnick to note that the new poor law was a 'bachelor'.[2]

Dickens Responds

The future of an illegal child was so grim that even Dickens backpedalled from it in the last pages of *Oliver Twist*. Right up to the last instalment of that serialised novel, readers had believed that Oliver was born out of wedlock. Then, at the eleventh hour, Dickens pivoted and made Oliver the child of a secret marriage. Mr and Mrs Bumble were found to have destroyed the evidence of his legitimacy. Dickens himself never overcame his repulsion to unwed motherhood. In the end, he could not bring himself to make Oliver the product of such wantonness, even though *Oliver Twist* is a thorough condemnation of the new poor law in every other way.

Many Victorians were justly outraged by the harshness of the new poor law. In writing *Oliver Twist*, Dickens channelled that anger. His own righteous indignation combined with what he knew of the workhouse system from living right next door to one of these facilities. It also combined with the haunting memory of his own, admittedly brief, sentence to child labour. *Oliver Twist*, Dickens's second novel, was written in a year, the product of working well into the night. Compared to some of Dickens's later novels, it is brilliantly concise. Later on, his by-the-instalment contracts led to windy digressions and hyper-detailed descriptions of indoor settings. But *Oliver Twist* was driven by a strong and urgent sense of injustice.

The new poor law was repealed in 1948, ten years after the publication, as a whole book, of *Oliver Twist*. History cannot draw a straight line between the novel and the repeal of a wicked law. By no means was Dickens's voice the only voice raised against the new poor law. But when we look for the influence of art on history, the beacon of *Oliver Twist* burns bright. It bravely and clearly exposed an unfair system, and that system was reformed in its wake. *Oliver Twist* remains iconic as a truly influential social novel.

Inspired by *Oliver Twist*, this book will look at the larger issue of childhood poverty in England in the nineteenth century. Though the new poor law stands almost alone as one of the most vicious public policies ever deliberately implemented, it did not invent poverty. As we shall see, in upcoming pages, life was cruel to poor children before, during, and after the advent of the new poor law. We will consider the example of Charles Dickens himself who underwent a period of abuse as a child labourer, the orphan Robert Blincoe, the trafficked Eliza Armstrong, and the unnamed Oliver Twists of the Victorian age: chimney sweeps, matchstick makers, and forced emigrants.

Chapter 1

Boy Interrupted: Dickens's Childhood Twist

C harles Dickens's father, John Dickens, has been the butt of biographical jokes and witticisms for the past 150 years, at least. The great novelist himself was perhaps the first to turn his father into a comic character. In *David Copperfield*, it is generally agreed, the character of Wilkins Micawber is based on John Dickens. Like Dickens, Micawber is a basically honest and good-natured man, though deeply flawed by his inability to manage his finances. The important similarities between the real-life Dickens and Micawber are the time both served in debtors' prison and the good will of the wives who stood by them.

But no one could have been harder on John Dickens than Charles Dickens's biographer Gilbert Keith Chesterton, himself an accomplished fiction writer, though not as prolific as Dickens.

Chesterton paints the elder Dickens as a man who would have slowly and painfully dragged his family into poverty and ignominy, had he not had the unearned good fortune of producing Charles Dickens: 'if they had not been lifted in the air by the enormous accident of a man of genius, the Dickenses, I fancy, would have appeared in poorer and poorer places … until they melted into the masses of the poor.'[1]

Though Chesterton admits that the senior Dickens was an unusually good-natured man, the Father Brown creator faults him for the neglect of his son's education: 'He exhibited toward his son that contradiction in conduct which is always shown by the too thoughtless parent to the too thoughtful child. He contrived at once to neglect his mind, and also to over-stimulate [sic] it.'[2]

Chesterton's determination to trash the novelist's education rather inexplicably ignores the fact that any different education would not have produced Charles Dickens. It might have produced a beloved Oxford don or a popular member of Parliament. But history would have lost the novelist who produced *Great Expectations* and *Bleak House*.

Chesterton harshly judges John Dickens for what Chesterton saw as a laissez faire approach to educating his son Charles. Instead of instructing Charles, John preferred to be entertained. To that end, he required Charles to sing memorised songs and tell stories to him. Charles was only too happy to oblige.

At an early age, the boy Charles Dickens learned how to narrate, and his narrations were honed by the informal feedback of his family. His family doubled as his first audience: 'almost as soon as he can toddle, he steps into the glare of the footlights', is the way Chesterton phrases it, adding, 'He never stepped out of it until he died.'[3]

Instead of solely absorbing knowledge, Dickens was always in the process of conveying information, usually in the form of a performance. Chesterton preferred to believe that the genius of Charles Dickens sprang up out of nowhere, a mystery of the universe. But, in fact, his childhood of uncensored reading and spontaneous performance was an ideal nursery for perhaps the greatest novelist of the nineteenth century. Indeed, John Dickens's only real claim to fame (and the notability on which his Wikipedia article uneasily sits) is that he was a mostly irresponsible father to the great Charles. Still, his irresponsibility had unintended consequences which were, in this instance, transformative.

Charles's formal education was typical of the middle class into which he was born. He and his sister Frances attended a 'dame school' above a shop. Such schools were akin to the one-room schoolhouse. They were presided over by one teacher, typically a woman, and they were hyper-local. The classes had the advantage of being small. Prior to this, Dickens's mother had taught him to read, beginning at a very early age.

In fact, the childhood of Charles Dickens was very nearly idyllic, up to the point when it was not. From birth to his twelfth birthday, Charles had been a happy and imaginative child. The Dickens family had a decent-sized library in the garret of their home. There, Dickens exercised his fervid imagination freely and with little of the supervision that turns children into dull adults. He was allowed to read racy novels like *Robinson Crusoe*, *Gill Blas*, *Humphrey Clinker*, *Tom Jones*, as well as the entire *Arabian Nights* at a very young age.

Until his world came crashing down, he had little idea that his mother, father, and seven siblings sat on the knife point of poverty and had done so for at least a year. Like all children, Dickens had no basis of comparison. He had been fed, kept reasonably warm, and received the warm, if undisciplined, attention of his father and mother. Life for such a child is often happy, or even blissful.

When he heard the word 'deed', spoken in hushed tones, he had no idea that document was his father's hail Mary attempt to come to terms with his creditors. Like debtors today, John Dickens tried to 'restructure' his financial obligations. But unlike today's corporations, Dickens's creditors did not have to accept 80 pence on the pound and call it good enough, or give him more time. One creditor had had enough: the baker, James Kerr. In munching on Kerr's bread, the Dickens family had accrued a consolidated debt of £40 and 10 pence. Before we sneer at the pettiness of the debt, let us understand that sum. In the early twenty-first century, that would be approximately £3,385.

Other attempts had been made to steer the Dickens family back to solvency. Dickens's mother, Elizabeth, bravely tried to start up a school. She had, after all, taught her own children to read. And her children were remarkable, at least partly as a result of that education. She was an educated woman. The idea that she might bring recognisable value as a teacher was not unreasonable. To the end of starting up a school, the Dickens family hazarded some capital expenses. Unfortunately, when no students enrolled, those expenses deepened the financial hole in which John Dickens found himself.

At that point in history, debt was an imprisonable offence. John Dickens had used up all Kerr's reservoirs of compassion. Dickens must do time in Marshalsea prison.

Marshalsea was notorious and scary. It was renowned for holding captive romantic villains such as sailors who broke the laws of the sea, endangering whole ship crews, and political traitors. These notorious scoundrels made up less than half the prison population, however. The other half simply owed money. In fact, half the inmates in all of England's prison system were people who could not pay back their loans.

When the breadwinner of the Dickens family went to Marshalsea, the disposition of the children tells us numerous unfortunate things about the nineteenth century.

Charles's older sister, Frances, had already been accepted to a prestigious music school and her tuition had been paid, which had further enlarged the financial hole into which the family had been steadily falling. As a consequence of that pre-paid tuition, her education continued uninterrupted while Dickens Sr. did time. Charles would struggle, for life, with the disparity between his sister's fate and his own during his father's interment.

Prior to that interment, Charles had not gone to school for months. He had been writing in secret, mostly making character sketches of old and eccentric people he met. But either the family was unaware of this work or they thought little of it.

In what happened next, to Charles, we can see the stark contrast between the nineteenth and twenty-first-century conceptions of childhood. No one was particularly shocked when it was proposed that the 12-year-old boy go to work at a factory and earn 6 shillings a week toward putting the family back on its feet. In fact, this idea was put forward by a friend of the family, James Lamert, who owned a boot blacking factory. And the proposal was gratefully accepted by the Dickens family.

It is obvious from Dickens's writings that he had high aspirations for himself as a child. He hoped to go to Cambridge despite the fact that no one in his immediate or extended family had gone to any university, much less one of that distinction. He felt a power within himself that had not received acknowledgement from his parents or siblings when he was twelve.

Instead of prepping for Cambridge, he found his education discontinued indefinitely and himself thrust into stultifying adult manual labour. He was assigned to put labels on the bottles of blacking substance. There were, no doubt, more dangerous and unpleasant jobs in the factory, but Dickens never got over the nightmare of labelling bottles. When, as an adult, he looked back on this time in his life, it is the sound of rats that forms the soundtrack to the memory. The factory itself was a 'crazy, tumble-down old house … literally overrun with rats. Its wainscoted rooms, and its rotten floors and staircase, and the old grey rats swarming down in the cellars, and the sound of their squeaking and scuffling coming up the stairs at all times.'[4] Dickens was also offended by the dirt and the bleak view of coal barges making their ponderous way down the river. He worked ten-hour days.

Lamert had promised to provide Charles with some education during the lunch hour, but that promise went mostly unfulfilled. At first, out of some recognition that Dickens was not cut out for manual labour, he got to work in the 'counting house,' i.e. the rooms where the money was handled. But that would not last either. Soon, he found himself in the warehouse where other boys were working, attaching labels. These boys appear to have been kind enough, but they were rough-speaking and acting, and the imaginative, mostly cloistered Dickens felt degraded in their company. Dickens's biographers often make out that he was an egoist who felt superior to these other child labourers, but it seems more likely that he just felt superior to the work itself, and the culture shock of working with non-readers added to his unease. Chesterton refers to this time in Dickens's life as a 'bestial nightmare'.[5]

He missed his brilliant sister. But when he got an evening off to see her receive an award at the Royal Academy of Music, his self-pity got the better of him. It seemed like the end of the world. Here was his sister getting the artistic recognition she deserved while his talent languished: 'I could not bear to think of myself – beyond the reach of all such honourable emulation and success. The tears ran down my face. I felt as if my heart were rent. I prayed when I went to bed that night to be lifted out of the humiliation and neglect in which I was.'[6]

Dickens was often hungry during this time, removed as he was from a household with regular meals and a grocery list. His only companionship was that of other boys who worked at the factory, especially Bob Fagin, after whom Dickens would later name the villain of *Oliver Twist*. He was separated from his family, his books, his freedom, forced to spend hours a day in repetitive, unimaginative tasks, robbed of part of his childhood.

It did not help that Charles was small for his age and plagued with an undiagnosed health condition that manifested as pain in his side. His happiness improved when he was able to move closer to Marshalsea and eat breakfast and dinner with his family. The horrors of spending time in a debtors' jail paled in comparison with the loneliness he had felt.

Despite his loneliness and isolation, Charles never complained at work. He kept his head up, let no one know that his father was in prison, and showed no signs of the unhappiness in his heart.

The poverty, occasional hunger, and repetitiousness of his existence at this time were not the main sources of disappointment. No, what Dickens felt the most, right there at 12 years of age, was his squandered potential. With every label he applied, he heard the clock ticking away on his dreams of grand achievement. That Cambridge degree and the honour that education could bestow were slipping away. He could feel it.

Though it loomed large and eternal in Charles Dickens's memory, the purgatory of manual labour was short-lived. An elderly family member died, leaving John Dickens enough money to pay his debts. He was released from Marshalsea, and, soon enough, Charles went back to school, though he never attained the level of formal education he had hoped for.

Years later, he would avenge himself on his father by turning him into the self-dramatising Wilkins Micawber. After serving his time in debtors' prison, Micawber became a self-proclaimed expert on borrowing and its perils in *David Copperfield*: 'Annual income twenty pounds, annual expenditure nineteen pound and six, result happiness,' Micawber pontificates. 'Annual income twenty pounds, annual expenditure twenty pound ought and six, result misery.'

Neither Dickens nor his many biographers have thought to cut John Dickens a little slack, given the absence of family planning technology in the Victorian age. Chesterton sees J. Dickens as a man doomed, by his superficial character, to let his family down in some meaningful way. What he and Charles overlook is how well Dickens Sr. was holding it all together on a clerk's salary when he had only five children. Micawber could just as accurately have said, 'Annual income twenty pounds, five children, result happiness; annual income twenty pounds, seven children, result misery.'

How many Victorian families, one might well ask, fell into poverty when the numbers of children exceeded the financial resources? And how many of those families might have been sustainable if the growth of the family could have been managed by something other than the will of God?

It must be noted that the children Dickens later wrote about had much worse lives. Dickens was not struck with a fatal illness, like Little Nell. Nor was he forced to pick apart oakum as was Oliver Twist. No, Dickens's days were spent putting labels on bottles. He did not work directly with the shoe polish (called 'black' or 'blacking') that was produced in that factory.

Yet the experience of going to work at 12, losing daily access to his family, leaving his childhood home, and above all fearing that he would, on account of this setback, never achieve the potential he felt in himself scarred Dickens. The brevity of this passage in his life did not eclipse its enormity. Today, we would probably label this a traumatic event; the important thing about trauma is that it doesn't have to take years.

One sign of trauma is that Dickens never, but once, spoke or wrote directly about his father's imprisonment or his exploitation as a factory boy. This should not surprise us too much. Many famous people have chosen silence about bad patches in their lives, especially childhoods fraught with deprivation. The exceptions illuminate the rule.

It is possible that, in never speaking of his father's imprisonment, he was protecting the reputation of his family, even the reputation of John

Dickens, a man Dickens both adored (mostly as a child) and despised (mostly as a grown-up).

But it seems even more likely that Dickens didn't want to relive the experience of exile by speaking or thinking about it. To do so would be to relive the fear, the terrible fear that this horrible repetitive job would be his life, these boys who had never turned the pages of a book, his social circle. The fear that the developing fire of imagination and observation brewing inside him would be stifled under the ceiling of a factory warehouse.

As an adult, he spoke of his boyhood interruption once and only once, to his friend and later biographer John Forster. 'My whole nature,' he told Forster, 'was so penetrated with grief and humiliation ... I often forget in my dreams that I have a dear wife and children; even that I am a man and [I] wander desolately back to that time in my life.'[7]

And, like all great novelists, he put his trauma, his loneliness, his fear and disappointment into his books. If he had never lived with deprivation, would Dickens ever have painted such poignant portraits of lost children?

This period of boyhood interruption would be the experience that Dickens would exorcise, again and again, in novels about abused and abandoned children: the eponymous David Copperfield, Pip of *Great Expectations*, and, above all, Oliver Twist.

Oliver represents thousands, perhaps tens of thousands, of children who were trafficked in the broad light of day, put to strenuous work, starved, housed in wretched workhouses, and left vulnerable to the influence and abuse of society's worst elements.

The following chapters will examine some of the real Oliver Twists by name, though most of them lived and died in obscurity. Robert Briscoe, Eliza Armstrong, and George Elson are among the rare names that have survived down the 150 years since *Oliver Twist* hit the bookstands, one instalment at a time.

Dickens may or may not have known the names of these children who embodied the social injustices he wrote so poignantly about. In his mind, the very first real-life Oliver Twist was himself.

Chapter 2

Roger Blincoe:
Workhouse and Factory Survivor

Literature is in love with orphans. Dickens was not the first writer to focus all his talent for pathos on the unparented. Charlotte Brontë's Jane Eyre was an orphan. Emily Brontë's Heathcliff was an orphan. In France, we have the orphan Cosette in *Les Miserables*. The genre of fairy tales is built on imaginary orphans: Peter Pan, Snow White, Rapunzel.

With her usual razorlike perception, that eminent Victorian Florence Nightingale scoffed that literary orphans were the only young women afforded any freedom over their own destinies. Well brought up young ladies, she complained, had to fight with their families to establish any identity or destiny of their own. She would have been familiar with imaginary orphans such as Jane Eyre, Heathcliff, Cinderella, and, possibly, Moll Flanders. In each of these literary lives, the absence of parents allows the young hero or heroine a freedom to pursue daring action that he/she would never have had in a comfortable middle-class childhood with two parents.

Notwithstanding parents whose solicitations interfere with the dreams of the mighty, the reality for English orphans in the nineteenth century was nowhere near so liberating as Nightingale imagined. In her book, *Orphan Texts*, Laura Peters theorises that the Victorians used orphans as scapegoats to distract attention from the obvious deficits in family life. For Victorians, family was a sacred institution, but, according to Peters, unsustainable as a symbol of 'legitimacy, race, and national belonging'.[1] By demonising and isolating orphans, the Victorian family re-established its credentials, Peters posits:

the orphan, as one who embodied the loss of family, came to represent a dangerous threat; the family reaffirmed itself through the expulsion of this threatening difference. The vulnerable and miserable condition of the orphan, as one without rights, enabled it to be ... treated as such by the very structure responsible for its care.[2]

Peters is correct in asserting that Victorian orphans were basically punished for something that was in no way their fault. And the institutions that were assigned to care for orphans – the workhouses, parish houses, employers, nurses, and foster parents – were often inexplicably abusive. Upon reaching adulthood, even the most gentle and obedient orphan would have difficulty finding work. Employers openly discriminated against orphans, especially those who had been raised in workhouses, even though workhouses produced highly socialised children. The more dangerous orphans grew up on the streets or in rookeries.

And why were there so many orphans in Victorian England? Frequent crop failures and inflation brought many families to the knife edge of starvation. Many agricultural workers were displaced by industry and enclosure. The lack of a consistent safety net for poor families also contributed to the orphan problem.

Orphan ranks were swelled by children who had one or even two parents who were, quite simply, unable to care for their children. In the Western world today, it is unimaginable that a child with no parents in evidence might wander the streets for weeks, eating garbage, with no intervention. At the very least, such an occurrence would make headlines. But in the Victorian era, especially in the cities, victims of poverty frequently abandoned their children to scavenge for themselves. Or they dropped them off at a church or workhouse, hoping for the best.

According to Peters, on a single day in 1844, there were 18,261 children living in the workhouses of England and Wales. In 1862, this number had increased to 40,557. Interestingly, only about half of these children were actually deserted or orphaned. The rest had been dumped there by parents or guardians who could not or would not undertake the financial burden of raising a child.[3]

The real-life person of Robert Blincoe embodies the worst social problems of the Victorian era. First, he is a despised and illegitimate orphan, then an abused workhouse boy, then an exploited factory boy. It is a miracle that he made it to 68.

There is no absolute proof that Dickens had read the memoir of Robert Blincoe before sitting down to write *Oliver Twist*. But the parallels between Blincoe's life and the fictional Oliver's abound. Both Oliver and Blincoe were orphans in the St Pancras workhouse. Both were put to work at very tender ages. For both boys, their first work was pulling apart rope fibres to produce the raw material for oakum. Both were starved by the people who were charged with their care. Both overcame adversity and found love and success.

The child welfare advocate and journalist John Brown interviewed Blincoe and then wrote Blincoe's biography. This was published in 1828, in five instalments in the *Lion*, a newspaper owned by Richard Carlyle. In 1832, it was reissued as a pamphlet. Dickens, whose star as a novelist was rising, would have had access to this widely circulated story before he started writing *Oliver Twist* in 1837. These parallels have led some people to call Robert Blincoe 'the real Oliver Twist', which is also the title of John Waller's biography of Blincoe.

Scholars have noted that the story of Robert Blincoe's life as told to John Brown and subsequently published in the *Lion* is unlikely to be an exactingly accurate biography. The problems are there for all to see. Blincoe's adult memory of things that happened when he was 4, 5, and 6 are far too vivid. Also, the story frames Blincoe as a child imbued with unacknowledged greatness. His envy of the lowest free person outside the workhouse walls, the depictions of his attempted escapes and rebellions aim to glorify him as a uniquely sensitive and imaginative individual.

Perhaps it is crass to say it, but there is nothing in Blincoe's story that proves he was extraordinary. The height of his achievement was to become a cotton manufacturer. The value of his story lies, not in any personal grandeur, but in his ability to represent the dispossessed of his era.

As readers of Blincoe's life, we must be aware of a tendency to glorify while also crediting the story as told to John Brown as true in its broad strokes. Through painstaking research into parish documents, twenty-first-century biographer John Waller was able to verify many of the facts in the original memoir. The result is Waller's recent biography of Blincoe, titled *The Real Oliver Twist*.

It really doesn't matter whether Dickens's Oliver is partly inspired by Blincoe's memoirs. *Oliver Twist* is not meant to be the story of only one boy. It is meant to expose a system of abuse and cruelty toward England's children. Similarly, Blincoe's biography was meant to represent all the children who, like Blincoe, grew up in workhouses, then were sent to work, often before the age of 10, in dangerous factories and other work environments. It would be more accurate, therefore, to say that Blincoe is one of many Oliver Twists born into a nineteenth-century industrial era that often used children to build the fortunes of others by subjecting them to harsh hours and severe dangers.

Childhood in the Workhouse

Robert Blincoe never knew who his parents were. He had vague memories of a kind female in his life, previous to his stay in the parish house. But he was deposited with the St Pancras parish, outside London, at the age of 4.

The world he was born into was a bleak one. Life expectancy for the urban working-class poor was approximately 17. The industrial revolution was well underway, but the laws which would eventually temper its abuse of factory workers were either not yet drafted or unenforced. Blincoe was one of around thirty-five other orphans who had made the workhouse their home. He was unique, however, in having no connection to the surrounding community. Some of the workhouse children still had living parents who were too poor to care for their offspring. St Pancras was not the worst workhouse because parents were allowed to visit their children. Even the other true orphans had extended family members – aunts, uncles, cousins – and friends who would drop by and enliven the dull workhouse existence.

Like Oliver, Blincoe and the other children were put to work picking apart the ropes that were used to make oakum. Oakum repurposed old ropes which, when reduced to fibres, were mixed with tar to make a kind of mortar. This material was most often used to patch cracks and holes in boats and ships, but it could be used to patch walls and other structures.

Picking oakum was dreadful work, and the children worked twelve-hour shifts. The fibres of the rope left their fingers sore and bloody. When workhouse orphans could not be involuntarily recruited for picking oakum, such work was frequently assigned to hardened criminals fulfilling their prison sentences. The saving grace of the St Pancras workhouse was that work was sporadic. The able-bodied poor living outside the workhouse would frequently snatch up any available piece work or temporary employment, leaving the children of the workhouse to be children for days on end.

Nor were the children of St Pancras systematically starved as children would be later under the new poor law. Their diet was generous for the Victorian age. They got three meals a day, with decent amounts of protein, including milk, cheese, beef, broth, and weekly lamb. Butter and sugar made frequent appearances at the crowded workhouse tables, and those fundamental flavour makers, vinegar and salt, were consistently rationed. At Christmas they even feasted on roast beef and plum pudding, the historic symbols of English prosperity. They had sufficient nutrition to support both health and the fast growth rates of children. These well-fed workhouse residents were the envy of their slightly older peers working fourteen hours a day in factories, fuelled with ungenerous portions of bread and porridge. Rudimentary hygiene was supported at St Pancras, with inmates receiving a ration of soap on a regular schedule.

The children also received the rudiments of an education, presumably when they were not working twelve-hour shifts pulling apart ropes. This education consisted of the traditional reading and arithmetic. If Blincoe began his education at the age of 4, immediately upon being interned at St Pancras, he would, it follows, have had three years of desultory schooling, maybe more. On Sundays, the workhouse residents received compulsory religious instruction. Whether this was a kindness depends on the value you place on religion. At least the children could count on a couple of hours a week during which they would not be thrashed or made to pick oakum.

And that is approximately where the neglectful benevolence ends. The workhouse was, in so many other aspects, a full-on horror show. A building that might have been considered at capacity housing forty-five people was bursting with 450. Children at St Pancras slept five to a bed, and their beds were always infested with bugs. The building sat over what was effectively a sewer. Water from the streets ran into the basement which frequently overflowed the floorboards of the residential area. The smell of the place would have been unbearable to anyone who didn't reside there. The residents, of course, became inured to it.

The building itself was unstable. It featured rotting wood and a lack of support beams. Inspections carried out after Blincoe's residency found that support walls had actually been removed, presumably to accommodate the over-capacity population.

The governors charged with overseeing the conditions at the workhouse lived in dread of an outbreak of contagion. It was nothing short of a miracle that, in the three years Blincoe lived at St Pancras, no epidemic started there and spread to the outlying region. Overcrowded, unsanitary dwellings are nurturing hosts of infection and disease.

Since any pandemic would naturally start at the workhouse, it made perfect sense to the town leaders to keep contagion confined there. When two men died under suspicious circumstances, their bodies were immediately transferred to St Pancras, to await a post-mortem. The men had been unloading a shipment of cotton from Spain. In the Middle Ages and later, imported fabric was one of the plague vectors. Blincoe and his fellow residents had some tense hours, wondering if they would contract the black death. Good fortune struck again when the local doctor examined the bodies and found the cause of death to be untransmittable pleurisy.

Despite the persistent belief in welfare cheats, there were few young or middle-aged adults in the workhouse, excepting those that worked there. Most of the residents were too old and infirm or too young and small to take jobs and set up households for themselves. The exceptions were the ten or so residents suffering from severe mental health deficiencies. These unfortunates were often tossed into workhouses because facilities that specialised in mental health were so few and far between.

Despite these horrific conditions, Blincoe steadfastly claimed, as an adult looking back on his childhood, that his greatest privation was the lack of freedom. The workhouse was a prison. For the elderly, the only way out was in a coffin. For the children, the only exit was a period of enslavement euphemistically framed as an 'apprenticeship'.

In idle moments, Blincoe would look out of the workhouse windows at the river below and at the free men, women, and children who passed by, going about their business. St Pancras was a tourist destination, so Blincoe saw the occasional day trippers. More often, he saw an urban mix of merchants, housewives, paupers, and labourers. He envied all of them, even the men who, at night, removed faeces from homes and businesses and transported it out of town in carts before the days of municipal sewer systems.

But the objects of Blincoe's greatest envy were the chimney sweeps. Boys not much older than Blincoe strutted with confidence down the streets, often singing out to advertise their availability for business. Blincoe had no idea how dangerous and toxic the life of a chimney sweep was. But it speaks to his frustration that such an existence looked like paradise. When the chimney sweep masters came to the workhouse to recruit apprentice sweeps, the other children were properly alarmed. But Blincoe put himself forward with enthusiasm, standing on tiptoe to make himself appear taller. He was, nevertheless, considered too small for that work. Considering the mortality rate for sweeps, one might say he dodged a bullet.

When adults reminisce on childhood, it is always tempting to make our childhood selves more extraordinary than they really were. So, it is possible that Blincoe did, to some extent, romanticise his longings for freedom. He may also have romanticised his longing for death.

In a rare outing, the children of St Pancras were rounded up and taken to a nearby clinic for smallpox vaccinations. Such vaccinations were still somewhat experimental and invariably a few of the vaccinated died when the inoculant proved as virulent as the disease. Still, considering how quickly an outbreak of 'the pox' could have decimated the workhouse population, the benefits of inoculation far outweighed the risks.

The mechanism of vaccination was extremely crude. Cuts were made in both upper arms of each child. Then the pus from a recent smallpox victim was smeared into the cuts. Later, it was discovered that you could simply scratch the inoculant into the top layer of skin, but the Victorians of St Pancras were not taking any chances, so the infected substance got smeared in like a sandwich spread. When it was working according to plan, the vaccinated patient would develop running, smallpox-imitating sores where the cuts had been made. In other words, he or she developed a low-dose case of smallpox. Since one can't get smallpox a second time, because of in-built immunity markers that the survivor develops, the patient was now immune to a worse, fatal case of smallpox.

Blincoe knew the dangers of this vaccine. Its risks would not have escaped the gossip grapevine at such a crowded workhouse, one where the nurses socialised with the inmates as equals, more or less. He knew, in other words, that the vaccination had a small chance of killing him. As an adult, looking back, he reported that he had hoped to be one of the few who died. He would have considered it a form of good fortune to die rather than continue the imprisoned, overcrowded life he had been dealt. The only reason to be sceptical of this report is that children are rarely aware of how bad their environmental circumstances are.

They have no basis of comparison. This in no way invalidates the fact that Blincoe, as an adult, experienced his childhood in such a way.

Despite the crowding, the lack of outdoor recreation, the bed bugs, and the itching, Blincoe's years in the workhouse were the best years of childhood that he remembered. Things were about to get much worse.

Indentured Children

Circumstances combined to make life even more precarious for the children of St Pancras. A food shortage, brought on by harvest failure, had doubled the price of bread over three years. It didn't help that England had recently engaged in a costly war with France. These factors led directly to runaway inflation, and the parish found itself suddenly responsible for many more poor people than in the years previous. Some of these unfortunates got shoehorned into the workhouse. Others got by on a combination of more informal charity and pawning their furniture.

Wards of charity were always the first victims of inflation and food shortage. The growth of a local poor population has always struck fear into the hearts of the wealthy. 'They outnumber us, what is to stop them from killing us?' was the interior monologue of many wealthy manor squires. They had not seen a barrage of 'eat the rich' Facebook memes, but their emotional response to rising poverty mostly centred on their own best interests. (What is surprising is how few times in history the poor have actually risen up to kill the rich and eat, well, not their bodies, but the resources of the murdered. In England, the dangers of poverty have always been borne, almost exclusively, by the poor.)

The care of St Pancras's inmates had become exponentially more expensive. The cost of feeding them was higher, and now there were more of them. Community leaders started looking into how to offload some of their poorest parishioners. And who makes an easier target of dishonest exploitation than a child? To that end, workhouse administrators eagerly met with mill owners to arrange what were very euphemistically called 'apprenticeships' for the workhouse children. To the Victorian ear, the words 'child labour' did not have the ring of horror. They simply did not see anything wrong with children under 12 working full-time. Even gruelling physical labour was business as usual for poor children.

By today's standards, what happened next to Roger Blincoe and many of his peers is not something we can call 'child labour', unfortunately. Today, it would be called 'human trafficking'. Of all the abuses that Victorian children were subjected to, indenture without consent had to be among the worst.

History and Culture of Indenture

To understand Blincoe's 'apprenticeship', we must pause and consider the history and nature of indentureship. Indentured servitude was invented in the British colonies, specifically the state of Virginia, in 1619. Free, but desperate men and women would sometimes indenture themselves in exchange for passage to 'the new world' which meant North America or, later, Australia, in general. Under their contracts, these indentured servants would work a period of years, with no salary, for those who had paid their ship fare.

This system was a nightmare for many and a pathway to fame and success for a few. The architect William Buckland was one immigrant to the 'new world' whose risk paid off. Buckland voluntarily entered into indentured servitude at the age of 21. During and after his indentureship, he designed several buildings that are now under historic preservation protections in and around Annapolis, Maryland. He also married and had four children. Buckland represents the happy face of the indenture coin. For a man with health, drive, talent, and education, risking a one-way voyage to the new world was the nineteenth-century equivalent of space travel. The colonies were the Victorians' final frontier, an opportunity to make a name and a dent which would be impossible to make in the old world, trammelled as it was with an overabundance of drive, talent, and education.

Indentured servant Sally Brant represents the less happy side of that coin. Indentured at the age of 10, Brant was truly a servant-of-all-work. During the farm season, she was out in the fields, planting and harvesting. When not needed there – because plants do most of the work of growing plants – she performed as a maid for her family, Elizabeth and Henry Drinker. Brant even won Elizabeth's grudging acknowledgement that she was a good worker. However, indentured servants were, by contract, supposed to be asexual. Brant, who had been indentured as a child, turned out not to have a gift for celibacy.

She angered her employers by becoming pregnant out of wedlock. The mixed-race baby she produced, along with her refusal to demonstrate any shame about it, further infuriated her colonial masters. She had no difficulty identifying the child's father as Joe Gibbs, her master's driver, a man of African descent. She also gave her baby Gibbs's surname. It seems likely that Sally would have married Gibbs, if the terms of her indenture had allowed her to marry. They did not.

The Drinkers exacted some revenge against Sally by making sure she had minimal contact with her newborn. The baby got passed from one wetnurse to another so that Sally could keep working. Even though her baby died at seven months, the Drinkers invoked their right to lengthen her servitude because of what it cost them to hire wetnurses. Despite these unpropitious beginnings, Sally was freed at the age of 18, married a successful barber, had three more children, and, now, a Wikipedia page dedicated to her plucky ability to survive.

Over time, indentured servitude morphed from being the last resort of the desperate to being a punishment for the delinquent. English men and women could escape debtors' prison by indenturing themselves. In this way, they repaid their debt with free labour. It was a situation not unlike washing dishes to pay for your meal at a restaurant. Similarly, convicted criminals could agree to an indentureship, usually overseas, as an alternative to execution or a lengthy prison sentence.

Many historians have noted the similarities between slavery and indentured servitude. In fact, the indentured were treated as slaves in many ways. Perhaps the most notable of these was the prohibition on both marriage and sexual activity of which Sally Brant fell afoul. The important difference between slavery and servitude was and always will be consent. Even the convicted murderer, sentenced to a London hanging, had a choice in the matter. He could be hanged or take his chances on a months-long journey overseas and an indentureship with an unknown master.

In the case of an indentured child, his or her parents could give consent and sign the documents. If one determinedly forces rose-coloured glasses up to one's eyes, one can believe that the parents were acting in their child's best interests. Perhaps this future was better than homelessness and starvation or life in a family of criminals.

However, that fine distinction did not exist for the children of the St Pancras workhouse who became indentured without their own consent or that of their parents. The workhouse authorities were not acting in loco parentis; these children were items in a budget they wanted to slash. So, they trafficked them.

Gonalston Mill

In 1799, William Charles Lambert personally visited the St Pancras workhouse to recruit children for indentured servitude at Gonalston Mill, the cotton mill he co-owned with his brother Francis. Their mill, near Nottingham, was in the remote village of Lowdham. In those days of water paddle power, such mills were necessarily located in rural spaces because they needed running water of the kind only a sizeable river could provide. As the industrial revolution expanded, rivers in the cities became unavailable. They were already fully used by other mills.

This is where the Lambert brothers had a problem. In the cities, there were generally enough poor and desperate adults to staff the machinery and work the long hours for poor pay that factory work provided.

In rural communities, however, it was difficult to find such labour. Even subsistence labourers were intolerant of the hours and the confinement. Farm hands would work a few days or weeks on a farm, then have time off. Such was not the case for factory workers, who worked six days a week with no vacations – ever.

Furthermore, paying fair wages was not conducive to maximising profits. It never has been. The Lamberts solved that problem by effectively imprisoning children and making them work fourteen hours a day.

The mechanism of indenturing children was to pay the new master a small sum for the support of the child. This money was supposed to ensure that the child would be fed and housed. However, this system was very liberally construed. Nothing prevented a presumed master from taking this money and then disappearing, leaving the apprentice to fend for himself. In such a case, the abandoned child had few recourses. If he still had parents, he could return to his now further impoverished family. Otherwise, he was likely to end up in a workhouse or dead of starvation.

The St Pancras workhouse paid the Lamberts 30 shillings for each apprentice that the Lamberts transported to their mill. It was a win/ win for everyone but the children. St Pancras had been paying four times that amount to feed, clothe, and house their wards. The Lamberts walked away from this deal with a tidy sum of capital and free labour for the term of the indentures. In Blincoe's case, his indenture was to last fourteen years, until he was 21. As an added inducement to the limited consciences of the St Pancras parishioners, it was promised that the boys would be taught to weave stockings and the girls would learn lace making, potentially valuable skills, if they had been learned. That never happened.

This was all perfectly legal. The elaborate lies told to the children were not strictly necessary. But it was desirable to keep the trafficked children quiet and conforming during the three-day-long journey north. So elaborate lies were, in fact, concocted.

Robert Blincoe and his peers who were apprenticed to the mill in Lowdham were told that they were going north in order to become ladies and gentlemen of wealth. They would ride horses, have expensive watches, and eat roast beef and plum pudding on a regular basis. This ruse was tailored, rather cleverly, to the children's limited exposure to affluence. Roast beef and plum pudding was something they had experienced during the Christmas holidays. Looking out of the workhouse window, they could see that the better-dressed people rode horses or horse-drawn carriages. They would have learned about watches from the wealthier staff members or visitors to the workhouse or, again, from looking out of the window.

Even more appalling, though, was the atmosphere of virgin sacrifice that the workhouse created on the day of the apprentices' departure. The children were dressed up in bright clothes, and the workhouse beadles also dressed in regalia. Family members and friends were invited to see the children off to their brilliant new lives. The only thing missing was the four-piece brass band.

Even so, at least two families had the judgement to save their children at the eleventh hour. We do not know the names of the two children who fell off the ranks of the recruited. But we do know that families desperate enough and poor enough to send their children into workhouse imprisonment suddenly found the means to care for their loved ones at home rather than send them into an exile of slavery.

The St Pancras apprentices were loaded, not onto a battalion of fine steeds, but into covered wagons. We do not know at what point the children discovered that they were not going to be transformed into ladies and gentlemen. It is possible that a few of them noticed that, instead of fabric coverings, the wagons in which they travelled featured impervious wood coverings like coffin lids and were bolted from the outside.

The trip took three days, with the wagons making their way over deeply rutted roads at a pace of a few miles an hour. The children were seated on hard wooden benches with no grab bars or seat belts. As a result, they were frequently thrown to the floor. They were already well bruised at the end of the first day. Several children decided, early on, that the price of becoming genteel was too high. They called out to the wagon drivers that they would like to return home now. However, no wagons mercifully turned back. They all kept moving, slowly, inexorably, down the road. Along the way, people that saw them and knew they were factory bound referred to them as 'poor wretches' and 'livestock'.[4]

Eventually, they arrived and the children were taken to what amounted to an employee dormitory and, eventually, fed dinner. If any illusions of gentility persisted, that dinner would have shattered them. The cuisine at the workhouse had been a culinary delight by comparison with the starvation diet that the Lamberts would now afford them. At the workhouse, they frequently had cheese, butter, and other decent, if cholesterol-ridden protein sources. Now, dinner would be rye bread and a porridge so thin that Blincoe described it as 'blue'.

The food was a shock, but so was the sight of the older 'apprentices'. They were unwashed, and they stank of the oil used to maintain the mill's machines. The boys were barefoot. Cotton fibres hung off their unbrushed hair. Their clothes were made out of the roughest fabric, and those clothes were coated in dirt.

More importantly, they were startlingly undernourished. Their complexions were bad, their hair dull, their affects defeated, and they had not an ounce of spare body mass. These seasoned apprentices had no interest in getting to know the new employees, but they wolfed down any scraps of bread that were left on the plates of the naïve.

This, then, not the gilded watches and horses he had been promised, was Robert Blincoe's future.

For six days a week, the 7-year-old Roger Blincoe's day would start at 5.00 am. A loud bell would startle and destroy any dreams into which he might have slid to escape his horrible waking life. On the first day this happened, Blincoe got confused and thought they were going to church. For what other reason could he have been so rudely rousted out of bed at such an unreasonable hour? One of the seasoned apprentices quickly disabused him of that notion.

The workers had exactly thirty minutes from the bell to dress, force down a breakfast – more porridge and rye – and travel to the mill. Blincoe found himself deployed as a 'scavenger'. This position was akin to chimney sweeping in that it was highly dangerous, and only children were small and nimble enough to do it. Also, children could be trained to do it where adults would prefer starvation on the street.

Scavenging involved running around the mill at high speed, collecting pieces of cotton that had fallen to the floor. Such stray pieces could clog up the equipment. Children were to go under the machinery and pick up pieces that had fallen close to the moving parts. If the child were not both dextrous and careful, he would get seized up by the various flywheels, rollers, spinners, and paddles involved in turning cotton into fabric. During his time at Lowdham Mill, Briscoe would see a girl get caught in a machine. Within seconds her bones were pulverised, and her blood splattered around the factory. She survived, miraculously, but with extreme lifetime disabilities.

So, if Blincoe were to survive his apprenticeship, he had to dodge the various moving parts of the machines all around him, roaring at decibels that could quickly bring on nerve deafness. Factory bosses quickly made it clear that children could not take a break, they could not even sit down for a few seconds to catch their breath. This 'no breaks' policy was enforced by bosses who were quick to hit or kick seven-year-olds and other children if they didn't stay moving.

After lunch, Blincoe had to work, nonstop, until 8.00 pm. That was on a good day, a fourteen-hour workday. Twice a month, mill workers had to break down and clean the equipment, and those days involved working at least fifteen hours. Sunday was the only day off, but it was not a leisure day, as church was mandatory.

Under these circumstances, the only logical thing to do is escape. Blincoe's plan was to make his way to London, on foot, and dining off whatever begging could bring. He was still naïve enough to believe that London authorities would listen to his testimony against the Lambert brothers and do something about the Lowdham Mill abuses. Blincoe then imagined himself going back to the easier life of a workhouse.

At first, Blincoe thought that he could convince some of his peers to join him, but none would. Their spirits were already too crushed. So Blincoe found himself alone on the road to freedom. He rightly calculated that his risk of apprehension would be on the road between

Lowdham and Nottingham. Locals would know all the children who had business on that road, and they would also know that mill workers had no time during the day for an outdoor stroll.

He was correct in that calculation. He made it out of the mill and past the village, no problem. Two miles later, he was tired and hungry, but still moving at a fast pace and keeping an eye out for any search party coming for him. It was another two miles to Nottingham, where he could blend in anonymously with a larger community, or so he hoped.

What Blincoe failed to calculate was that his employers had anticipated runaways and set up lookouts. Of course they had. Robert was apprehended by a tailor who grabbed him and locked him up. Hunger, fear, and fatigue combined to make Blincoe bow to capture with little resistance. He did, however vainly, try to tell the tailor about the abuses at the mill. Blincoe was brutally thrashed for his attempted escape. The tailor received his usual remuneration for the return of a runaway. It was a nice little sideline for him.

The parish governors who had sent their charges to Lowdham Mill were not good people, but they could be shamed. It happened that two of the children sent north with Blincoe – Fanny, aged 13, and Mary Collier, 11 – still had a living parent. The girls wrote to their mother, Susannah Collier, describing their work conditions, and begged her to do something.

This mother, poor as she had to be to put her children in a workhouse, somehow managed the trip to Nottingham. Blincoe biographer John Waller speculates that she walked those many miles.[5] She observed the factory conditions without alerting the Lamberts or the mill overseers. Then, back home in St Pancras, she confronted the workhouse authorities.

They responded by making a trip to the mill. When they arrived, unannounced, during dinner, it was immediately obvious that the children were poorly cared for. The adults could tell from the food on the plates, the workers' sallow skin, untended hair, and unwashed faces that these children were being abused, even by the lax labour standards of the day. Even if the Lamberts had declared a shorter workday on an emergency basis, and instructed the overseers to be kinder to their employees, there was no hiding the fact that their child workers were badly exploited. The children themselves did not rat out the Lamberts. They were, of course, far too terrified of the beatings they would receive in retaliation.

As a consequence of this inspection, a few minor amendments were made. The governor who had tolerated beatings was fired. The children got better food, including better sources of protein and a shorter workday. Perhaps the most important improvement was the construction of a new, roomier apprentice house with better ventilation. These small changes did give the children a better quality of life, but only for a few months.

At the end of that time, the Lamberts decided to close their mill and sell off its assets. This did not come as a result of improved conditions for their workers. The Lowdham Mill's water-powered machinery had quickly become obsolete in the wake of newer, better technology. Their mill could not stay profitable in competition with the coal-fired steam energy that had come into vogue and made it unnecessary to locate a cotton mill next to a river. The children who had been uprooted from their communities and lost their window for learning a trade or skill of any real value were not a factor in this decision. But the Lamberts had to do something with them, because dumping them by the side of the road was technically illegal. The managers of the Backbarrow Mill had tried that and had faced a parliamentary inquiry. The Lambert brothers asked apprentices who had any family back in St Pancras to write to them, asking to come home. Blincoe believes a few of his peers made it back to the south.

The Horrors of Litton Mill

The majority of the Lowdham Mill workers, however, had their indentures sold on to another cotton mill, this one owned by Ellis Needham, an even more ruthless capitalist than the Lamberts.

The Lowdham factory workers found themselves on another wagon, this one bound for Litton Mill in Miller's Dale in the Peak District. The mill and lodge sat on the Wye River. The beauty of the Peak District and the Wye have been praised by William Wordsworth and other nature lovers. But the children did not, could not, benefit from the beauty of their natural surroundings. They spent their days confined either within Needham's factory or in the nearby apprentice house where they slept three to a bed.

It seems likely, from the vantage of history, that Needham deliberately picked a really remote location for his mill. It was surrounded by forests and the soundtrack of the Wye sometimes blotted out any sweeter sounds afforded by the district's birds. The nearest human population lived in the tiny hamlet of Litton. And the only path between that hamlet and the mill was a steep trail that few hamlet residents wanted to navigate.

It must have been difficult for the children who worked at Gonalston Mill to imagine that life could get any harder. But it did. At this new factory, the food was starchier and even lower in nutrients. Notably, the porridge was made with water, not milk. As he reached puberty, Blincoe developed bowed legs, partly as a result of standing all day, but mostly from malnutrition. The oat cakes were often mouldy and sour tasting, and the rice pudding maggoty. Another staple of this diet was the same meal-based dumplings that Needham fed his pigs.

The workday was even longer, and the children had to eat their food while at their jobs, wolfing down bites in the moments when their hands left the machines. The Sabbath, so sacred to the Victorians, was frequently violated. On Sundays, after being assaulted with lessons in grammar and religion, the children were driven back to the factory to clean down the equipment. Needham got away with this because he was close friends with the local curate, a man of flexible morals himself. The two of them, Thomas Brown and Needham, formed a good old boy network of sorts. They maintained a tacit agreement to remain silent on each other's misdeeds and offer public recommendations as needed.

The children were allowed to wash themselves once a week – in the river. Instead of soap, they were issued oatmeal as a cleansing abrasive. Some of the more practical children with, it could be argued, superior survival instincts, ate their portion of hygienic oatmeal and then cleaned themselves with sand dredged up from the riverbed.

The children were tormented with head lice against which they were mostly powerless, especially with baths only once a week and no soap. A doctor that Blincoe refers to as both 'terrible' and a 'quack' was brought in for the worst cases of lice when the child did not know better than to complain. This doctor applied tar to the child's head, then, when it dried, he pulled it off, removing, yes, lice, hair, and an indiscriminate amount of the child's scalp. Interestingly, this 'pitchcapping' was also used as a torture method on the Irish, during their rebellion of 1798.

What should have aroused local concern, but did not, was the apprentice death rate at Needham's mill. Over thirty years, spanning the late 1700s and early 1800s, twenty-seven apprentices perished. To put that into perspective, only six employees died during that period at the nearby Cressbrook Mill.[6]

It appears that Ellis did quite a bit of advanced planning to mitigate the effects of a high apprentice death toll. His mill was located near the border between the Tideswell and Taddington parishes. Officially, his mill was located in Tideswell where Ellis maintained a residence. However, when his first batch of apprentices started showing signs of deterioration, he built a new apprentice house in Taddington. Taddington, then, became the official address of those apprentices. When one of their number became disabled, perhaps in an avoidable industrial accident, that child or teenager became the financial responsibility of Taddington under English poor laws. Ellis did not endear himself to the residents of Taddington this way. But doing so helped him protect his reputation in Tideswell which was of greater importance. When it came time to bury the children he had worked to death, he spread their bodies over three different cemeteries: the majority were buried in Taddington, but a few went to Tideswell and one was buried in the hamlet of Wormsloe where Ellis lived.

There were many ways a factory lad might die. The most obvious culprits were exhaustion from overwork and poor nutrition. A visiting doctor to Litton Mill went on record as saying the boys and girls needed more food and rest. Specifically, he recommended their diet be enriched with mutton, beef, and bread. When questioned why he did not report the mill conditions to the magistrate, the doctor indicated it would have been futile: 'the surgeon and magistrate were friends and guests of the master, and in the frequent habit of feasting with him.'[7]

That doctor was not the only one who noted conditions that were bad even in the context of an industrial revolution that was famous for inhumane factory conditions. Another doctor, Joseph Denman, was assigned to report to Parliament on factory conditions in his neck of the woods. Denman accepted Ellis's hospitality, but he did not wholly fudge his report. He noted that the apprentice houses were too crowded to be healthy or comfortable. He also noted that the privies were not 'well conducted', the children worked well into the night, and they were given no education.[8] Finally Denman gave away just how out of touch he was with factory realities by noting that there was no copy of the laws regulating factories anywhere on the premises. Did he really think that illiterate children, just trying to avoid being beaten, were going to take a break from their spinning to go read parliamentary law?

Denman's report clearly pointed to the Litton Mill as being the worst in the county. Nevertheless, it resulted in no improvements to Blincoe's life or to that of his factory peers. Nor did the next inspection accomplish much of anything. Magistrate Marmaduke Middleton was the next inspector charged with ensuring a minimal level of health and safety in the factories. Like Denman, he noted the diet and work schedule, but his statements betray no particular outrage. The children worked past nine at night, and their porridge was water based, providing no protein, said his report. What both Denman and Middleton missed was more important than what they reported. Neither inspector noted how many scars the children had, nor did they note Blincoe's deformed legs. It appears they made no effort to check the number of apprentices on the floor against the records. This allowed the Needhams to hide the children who had become disabled as a result of on-the-job injuries.

It is true that the Litton Mill workers were underfed and overworked. But the gravest danger at Litton was the gratuitous physical abuse.

And here there was a significant departure from the dreary life at Lowdham. In Lowdham, when the overseers beat children, it was out of fear that the overseers themselves would suffer if quotas were not met. At Litton, however, the punishments were sadistic. Torturing children was a form of entertainment that the administrative staff afforded themselves. Overseers would gather around to watch a child being abused in some new and, they thought, amusing fashion. Many of these supervisors had come up through the apprentice ranks. Statistics clearly show us that abused children often grow up to be violent, abusive adults. So, it should come as no surprise that children tortured as apprentices grew up to be torturers.

The punishments Blincoe describes in his memoirs are so horrible that readers may wish to conclude he allowed his imagination to run away with him. If only that were true. In fact, Blincoe's testimony about the cruelty at Litton has been verified by several other sources, including at least two apprentices who worked at that mill during the same period.

Children had to remove clothing to be beaten on their bare skin. From these beatings, Blincoe came away with welts so bad, they turned into ulcers. And the overseers were highly imaginative when it came to materials used to beat children. They did not confine themselves to sticks, but also used the rollers off the machinery, ropes, and belts. And not just plain leather belts, but belts that had metal buckles that would tear open the skin of a beaten child. Leaving a child not just bruised but with open, bleeding wounds was the norm. Another form of punishment was forcing children to eat candles, tar, spit – from the supervisor's mouths – and tobacco that had been mashed up in someone's mouth.

On more than one occasion, Blincoe had to stand on a cylinder with his hands tied behind his back. Then a piece of machinery would knock the cylinder out from under the boy, sending him sprawling and, simultaneously, trying to avoid landing on the nearby spindles which would have further disabled him.

One of Blincoe's jobs was to gather wayward cotton pieces that accumulated under the mill's machines. This was something he had learned to do at Lowdham, and he continued doing it at Litton. Children were needed for this work because they were small and fast. It was dangerous work because the mill was a vast network of constantly moving parts. So, the child gathering cotton had to do so while dodging various machines.

On one occasion, Blincoe was commanded to remove all the cotton under a machine called a 'mule' in one sweep, even though it was impossible to do this safely because gathering the cotton involved dodging the moving parts. Blincoe obeyed and, as the supervisors no doubt hoped, his head got jammed between two pieces of machinery. His skin was torn and blood vessels ruptured. Nevertheless, an overseer followed this with a beating.[9]

The children's ears were never safe. The abuses at Litton often focused on ears as both points that could be extremely painful and also points where injuries could be inflicted with less visibility. Picking children up by their ears and throwing them was only the beginning. Overseers also drove small nails behind ears and screwed hand vices on the children's ears. These vices weighed as much as 10 pounds each.[10]

Another way the staff at Litton amused themselves was to tie a child's hands and one ankle together and set the child hopping amidst the swiftly moving machinery, trying to avoid being crippled.

The name Robert Woodward comes up repeatedly in historical documents related to Litton Mill. He appears to have been the ringleader in the abuse of the child labourers. But the other overseers willingly participated in the abuses. On multiple occasions, Woodward tied Blincoe to a cross bar that moved through the air above a moving carriage. To avoid having his legs broken, Blincoe had to keep raising them above the machines.

Naturally, some of the Litton factory workers wanted to die. In a rare exception to the overall abject misery, one child found her freedom. This Phebe Rag was being constrained in leg irons to keep her from escaping. She threw herself into the nearby lake from a bridge and was retrieved from the water before she could die. Needham feared that her example might set off an epidemic of suicides. So, the fortunate Phebe got sent home to her parents.

On Sundays, when the apprentices were not ordered back to the factory after church for a furtive shift in violation of the Sabbath, they foraged like poorly managed livestock. The nearby woods did not afford much in the way of nutrition, but the apprentices did manage to snack on the fruit of wildflowers, clover, and leaves. A nearby farmer mostly turned a blind eye when these underfed workers stole his turnips. Some of the more enterprising amongst them would gather a small stash of turnips and hide them in the restroom for later consumption.

When Blincoe could escape the supervisory glare of Woodward and other overseers, he would raid the mill's compost/garbage pile for wilted cabbage leaves and the discarded peels of root vegetables. But the real carbohydrate score was the pig's trough. The children raided the Needhams' pig food so often that the pigs learned to set up a communal squeal and alert the swineherd when they saw the children coming.[11]

The Race Up the Slack: Justice Unmeted

At the age of 19, Blincoe was a damaged young man. He had been a well-proportioned child, even a little tall for his age. Now he was shorter than average because of the deformity in his legs. He was badly scarred with injuries that ranged from open gashes to welts that had blistered before healing. He was proverbially broken but unbowed.

He joined with three other Litton Mill employees, one of them an overseer, to demand shorter work hours. To that end, the four of them went on a strike, refusing to work. It should come as no surprise that this endeavour led to the punishment of the four workers. Three of them were thrown out of their mill-owned lodging and had to sleep in the woods. Blincoe sheltered with a friend.

The strike was technically illegal. And Ellis Needham took it so seriously that he showed up at the factory to beat the perpetrators himself. He assaulted Blincoe with his walking cane, then moved on to punish the others.

By this time, Blincoe had lived for many years in sight of the single narrow trail that led from the mill to the nearby village. As he moved, at night, from the mill to the apprentice house, he would have seen it there, leading to the unknown, appealing to his imagination. This little road was known to locals as the 'Slack'. Right after breakfast, on the day after his failed rebellion, Blincoe's patience broke. He took off up this trail, on foot, hoping to reach the home of Magistrate Henry Bache Thornhill. His aim was to blow the whistle on the Needhams and the conditions at their mill.

Blincoe knew nothing of English laws which did, in fact, prohibit at least some of the abuses that were taking place at Litton. But he knew that magistrates were supposed to stop wrongdoers. In this, he was, of course, a little naïve. Both Waller and even Blincoe's distant descendant, Nicholas Blincoe, have speculated that Blincoe's sense of self-worth came from a belief that he was descended from a clergyman who either could not or would not raise his own son. One imagines a spineless wallower in guilt, much like Arthur Dimmesdale, the joint sinner in Hester Prynn's scarlet letter. This speculation comes mostly from the fact that Robert's nickname at the workhouse was 'the parson' or just 'parson'.

However, it harms Blincoe's legacy to believe that he was motivated, not by an innate sense of justice, but by an unearned sense of entitlement. The son of a clergyman certainly deserved better than what he got at the Litton Mill. But so did each and every one of the other children indentured there. There will always be a few brave people who rise above their disadvantages to effect positive change. Without them, civilisation would have stagnated in caves. Why shouldn't Robert Blincoe be such a man of spirit?

Blincoe's escape from the Litton Mill was both short-lived and an education in how the rich protect each other from the consequences of their actions. When he arrived at Thornhill's home, a servant immediately diverted him to the Bull's Head Inn, a public house where policy issues would be heard the next day. Blincoe walked the distance back to the mill to sleep, then back to the village of Eyam the next day to plead his case before the magistrate and other witnesses gathered at the pub. Mr Cheek was there. He was a lawyer, acting on behalf of, amongst others, the Needhams. He wrote down Blincoe's testimony and read it to the other assembled magistrates. A hasty inquiry was made as to the whereabouts of the Needhams. At least one of them should have been at that meeting, but none were. An excuse was made for them. They were at the market. One magistrate, offended by Blincoe's effrontery, told him to get back to the mill. Blincoe immediately said that, if he went back now, he would be whipped.

At attendance at the Bull's Head was Marmaduke Middleton, the inspector who had reported bad conditions at Litton Mill. He seemed slightly more inclined to do something for Blincoe. At length, the magistrates dashed off a letter which effectively told the Needhams that they had to run their mill in accordance with the laws of the land. They gave this letter to Blincoe. With nothing else to show for his bravery, he returned to the mill with this letter and Middleton's promise to do something if, as Blincoe predicted, he was whipped upon his return.

Blincoe gave the letter to Woodward, who did not whip him. Woodward gave the letter to John Needham, Ellis's son, in whom the elder had invested much of the mill's management. It is an indication of just how little Victorian employers felt the hand of the law that John's first and only response to the letter was to, once again, whip Blincoe.

Blincoe naïvely believed the magistrates when they said the Needhams would not retaliate. So Blincoe again made his way up the steep Slack to throw himself on the mercy of Marmaduke Middleton. He arrived at that gentleman's house before Marmaduke was even awake. When he did finally meet with Blincoe, the magistrate informed the boy that he should not have come to him. He referred him back to the solicitor, Cheek.

Blincoe had picked up an amazing amount of information, considering how cloistered he was in the mill and apprentice house. Somehow he knew that Cheek had a conflict of interest in this matter, though he may not have known that Cheek was Needham's solicitor. The way he framed it to Middleton was, 'he is so thick with my master – they are often drinking together.'[12] Middleton cannot have been so naïve as a boy who had been confined to mills and workhouse, a prisoner, basically, from infancy. He took the small trouble of writing a letter to Cheek. Still trusting that the wheels of justice had not come to a standstill, Blincoe took possession of yet another letter and headed to Cheek's house. That man's home was twelve miles away, and Blincoe had no transportation but his feet and deformed legs. Spurred by a strong sense of mission, no doubt, Blincoe made the journey that same day, trudging through the rain.

It was there, at Whetstone Hall, that Blincoe's career as a whistleblower came to an anti-climactic end. He was greeted by a woman he recognised, Sally Oldfield, whose late husband had been a governor at the Litton Mill apprentice house. When she understood his business, Oldfield sat Blincoe down in the kitchen where his dreams of justice could die a slow, quiet death. Her advice: never 'go against thy master'.[13] To be fair, she also gave him something to eat and even some beer. Blincoe sat in Mr Cheek's kitchen for several hours during which time he saw no one but the ominous and disapproving Sally.

Blincoe was still under contract to work for the Needhams until he was 21. The English judicial system was a safety net with a great many holes in it, and Blincoe had fallen through several of them. Though indentured apprentices did sometimes run away from their employers, that was not an option for Blincoe. He had no family or friends who would take him in, no great skills that he could sell in the marketplace, no capital to make a start somewhere else.

He had to go back to the mill. He had to go back to work. Nothing had changed.

At the end of that brave adventure, Blincoe could do nothing about the overall conditions at the mill. He could do nothing for the many children that the Needhams were constantly importing as new apprentices. He could do nothing for his peers, the children who had, with him, first been trafficked to the Lamberts, then to the Needhams.

But he could do something for himself. Though he had accomplished nothing else, Blincoe had established that he was a squeaky wheel, someone who could not be tortured without resistance. When he got back to the mill, he explained to Woodward that he had met with the magistrates, and he had met with Cheek. He would, he went on to say, take no further legal action against the mill if the staff would refrain from beating him. This fake-it-till-you-make-it strategy actually worked. There were no more beatings.

Not for him.

Post-indenture

In 1813, Blincoe's period of indenture came to an end. It was inglorious. He had no money and no prospects, so he stayed on at the mill for another year, earning a small salary. Finally, he saved enough to try his luck in the larger world. He left Litton Mill with almost nothing. He had a few shillings, a few clothes. No horse, no letter of reference, no job or family to go to, no destination. He was visibly disabled. Strangers he met would ask him how he had got those injuries. The world could not be unkinder to him than it already had been. That did not mean that the road ahead would be smooth.

Blincoe spent the next several years in a series of poor-paying jobs. There was no Disability Discrimination Act to prevent employers from simply rejecting Blincoe on the grounds of his bad legs. However, there were many employers willing to exploit a handicapped man with few options and pay him much less than his work was worth. One such employer was John Clayton, who hired Blincoe to work as a spinner in the Mellor Mill. Blincoe worked there without complaint for several months until he learned that he was making substantially less money than his fellow spinners.

At this point, Blincoe committed the crime of Oliver Twist. He asked for more. Specifically, he went to see Clayton and ask for a raise. Clayton flew into a rage, refused, and said that he had hired Blincoe out of pity. Blincoe returned to work, thinking that was the end of that. But a few weeks later, he discovered that Clayton had hired someone new. Shortly thereafter, Blincoe was sacked.

This lesson in how little loyalty could exist between employers and their staff was repeated at Blincoe's next job. In Bollington, one Mr Lomax hired Blincoe to card cotton on the promise that a job as a spinner would open up in a matter of weeks. Blincoe found himself in a room with the other victims of workplace discrimination – women and children. Pulling cotton off cards to give to the spinners was unhealthy work. In an unventilated room – and they were mostly unventilated – cotton fibres would accumulate in the air and then get breathed into the lungs where they wreaked havoc, causing chronic illness and worker disability. When Blincoe failed to be promoted, as promised, he quit.

His next two jobs were at mills in Stalybridge, but here again he was hired only to card cotton, not as a more highly paid spinner. By 1815, he had left both jobs. He had pretty much exhausted his options in Stalybridge. It was time to try his luck in the big city of Manchester. There Blincoe found work in an eight-storey-high building called the New Mill, owned by brothers Adam and George Murray. Though the New Mill building impressively towered over every other structure in the neighbourhood, Blincoe found that the hours were irregular. He was not, it turned out, a full-time employee. Also the machinery heated up the rooms to an unhealthy degree. Sweaty workers became dehydrated and exhausted.

Blincoe left this job and took up a position at Robinson's factory. Once again, he was hired to card cotton. As part of his initiation, his fellow workers took him out and got him drunk – at Blincoe's expense. From this experience, Blincoe learned that he was neither a happy nor a resilient drunk. His hangover lasted for days, and he recommitted himself to sobriety.

Sobriety, of course, leads to reflection and even, in some people, the drive to better themselves. Blincoe was tired of carding cotton for pitiful wages. He had little education, and less opportunity to explore options while working night and day for a subsistence wage. But he had heard that people of humble origins, such as himself, could get ahead as self-employed waste cotton distributors. This involved obtaining so-called 'waste' cotton and selling it for use in coarse fabrics and as stuffing for padded clothes and pillows. Through this very narrow lens, Blincoe saw a way out of the cycle of poverty. But starting up a business, even a very small one, usually requires some investment. And Blincoe was unable to save money at his current low-paying salary.

So he took a chance, quit his job at the mill, and took a higher-paying position shovelling coal into a boiler. The higher pay came at a high cost to Blincoe. The hours were long and the work brutal, especially for someone with deformed legs. Yet Blincoe persisted in his goal to save enough money to start up his own business. To save on rent, he slept in the coal yard.

Blincoe did a good job of estimating how much money he would need to support himself while starting up his waste cotton supply business. He quit his job stoking the boiler and had a rough first year. His second year, however, he started making good money. The year 1819 finds him relaxing in a pub, with friends, and celebrating the christening of his neighbour's new baby. The days of working from dawn to night in social isolation, unknown, unrespected, were behind him.

Jane Austen famously wrote: 'It is a truth universally acknowledged, that a single man in possession of a good fortune, must be in want of a wife.' If she had had any experience of the nineteenth-century working class, she might have broadened that out to 'a single man with any income at all'. By the end of 1819, Blincoe was out of his financial hole and had amassed the grand savings of £5.

We return to his afternoon at the pub where he was enjoying the company of, among others, a neighbourhood butcher and a single woman by the name Martha Simpson. He was good enough friends with these two that the butcher joked that Blincoe and Martha should get married. Then they could celebrate a wedding as well as a christening. Blincoe, perhaps made bold by half a pint, said, 'If Martha will have me, I'll take her and marry her tomorrow.'[14]

Martha Simpson was one of those rare women who instantly recognises opportunity and seizes it without letting go. If she had written her memoirs, be assured your humble biographer would read them with great enthusiasm. But Martha was almost certainly illiterate, as evidenced by her making an X instead of a signature on her marriage documents. According to Waller, this was true of roughly 83 per cent of that era's brides.

Martha was of an age that allows men to dismiss her as 'a middle-aged spinster'.[15] Whether she saw herself that way or not, we know that she quickly accepted Blincoe's joking marriage proposal and then held him to it.

Blincoe had not gone to the pub that day to get engaged. He now found himself in a bizarre grey soup made up of two parts whimsy and one part lifelong commitment. Keep in mind, this young man's social skills had been formed in the worst environments of slave labour. The gentle arts of flirtation and dalliance were not his strong suit.

Still. He found his way. He repeated his proposal, this time more seriously. Martha again accepted. At this point, a small, impromptu betting pool rose up, with all the bets against the marriage. Blincoe was the only one who bet on himself. As he had always done.

He had several escape routes. He left the pub, claiming that he would apply for a marriage licence that very evening. He returned, demanding that Martha go with him. She agreed. He also claimed he did not have the £2 for the licence. Martha happened to have that sum on her.

They were married by Joshua Brooks, a clergyman whose reputation rested on marrying the local denizens en masse. He had much in common with the priests of Las Vegas. It was a June wedding, and it took place at Manchester Cathedral. Blincoe had won a leg of mutton and a few shillings in the wager. The boy who had walked over twenty miles in one day on deformed legs now hired a coach to take himself and his bride to church in state.

Eight years after leaving Litton Mill, Blincoe was a successful business owner, a married man, and middle-aged Martha had given him a daughter. She would give him two more children in short order. The fourteen-year or so age difference between Robert and Martha had not been an obstacle to starting a family. The unloved, orphaned workhouse boy would find himself the patriarch of a loving, sizeable family.[16]

The reader may find it gratifying to know that, while Blincoe's fortunes were rising, the Needhams' were failing. They had gotten into money lending without, it seems, attending to collateral. When a client defaulted, the Needhams needed a loan themselves. Over a period of a few years, they went bankrupt and lost both their estates.

Their poor money management was hardest, though, on their employees and apprentices. As their fortunes declined, the Needhams strived to steer clear of ruin by starving their employees. A contingent of these starving children escaped from the mill and made it all the way to London. There, authorities put them back into indenture, but this time, they were contracted to the Cressbrook Mill, owned by William Newton.[17] These children were the lucky ones, comparatively.

When the Litton Mill closed in 1815, the Needhams simply abandoned their workers. Because the apprentice house was in Taddington, eighty former workers were now the responsibility of that township, a township of approximately ninety families. Under the country's poor laws, Taddington was now obliged to provide for the penniless and unskilled factory workers. Naturally, the Taddington residents placed these charges with any employer who would take them, perpetuating a system in which employers had no checks on their abuses.

Documents show that ten people who became disabled while working for the Needhams had to throw themselves on parish charity. They did not last long on that charity. By 1818, the same year Blincoe became a successful self-employed businessman, all ten of these children were dead.

The Memoirs of a Working Man

In 1822, Blincoe met John Brown, the man who would turn him into a working-class hero. Blincoe's story resonated with Brown, who was a fierce reformer and advocate for the working poor. Brown has, probably with justice, been accused of twisting Blincoe's story to meet his own agenda. But Brown's story was and remains essentially true. From the relationship that developed between the two men, we learn something very interesting: proof that Robert Blincoe could read. In 1824, Brown gave Blincoe a copy of the memoirs and asked Blincoe to approve them. Blincoe did so, but wanted to add some more detail to the story, no doubt items that had been lost while the big picture was unfolding. Eventually, Blincoe's story would appear, serialised, in a periodical called the *Lion*. Later, it would be published as a book.

The subsequent course of Blincoe's life did not run as smoothly as sympathetic readers of his memoir would have hoped. Our hero was not content to remain a successful, but simple, middleman of waste cotton. He sold that business in order to go into cotton spinning. It was a risky move and one that might have paid off, if Blincoe had had just a little more money going into the venture.

He bought a 'mule', a spinning machine, and rented space in a mill. Doing this allowed him to make use of the mill's energy supply. Supplying energy was the main expense of operating a cotton mill. At this time, mills were either powered by fast-running rivers, such as the Wye, or they were powered by steam. The cost of erecting a mill was prohibitive, but small businessmen like Blincoe often rented space from larger mill owners.

Blincoe's luck fell quickly. His very first day as a self-employed cotton spinner, there was a fire in the mill. There were no deaths, and the mill as a whole remained viable. But Blincoe's machine was destroyed. He had failed to obtain insurance in advance, probably thinking there would be time for that when he started making money. This setback devastated the Blincoe family.

These events occurred after the writing of the memoirs, so some details are shrouded in mystery. We do not know, for instance, whether

Blincoe borrowed money to buy his spinner or whether he went into debt after the fire. He had a family and no income and may well have borrowed, after the fire, to keep them out of the workhouse.

In any event, Blincoe found himself in the unenviable position of being unable to repay his creditors. Where wealthier men, like the Needhams, were able to avoid the worst consequence of debt by declaring bankruptcy, Blincoe ended up in the Lancaster Castle gaol as a debtor. In this, he was less like Oliver Twist and more like Charles Dickens's father, John.

We do not know how Martha and the couple's children survived while Blincoe was in prison. Unlike Blincoe, though, Martha had family. They were in the picture when she married and more than likely they took her in when the Blincoe fortunes took a nosedive.

It should come as no surprise that Blincoe turned things around. The same drive that pulled him up from his destiny as a poorly paid cotton carder would save him from destitution again. We do not know how or when he was released from debtor prison. But documents show that the family was eventually reunited and living in Manchester.

By 1832, the Blincoes had not only recovered from their hardships, they were thriving. Robert had gone back to waste cotton distribution; he had also become a manufacturer of sheet wadding. The family owned a grocery shop in which Martha worked with one of her daughters. The Blincoes had three children altogether, and all of them received an education. The health of his children was a particular point of pride for Blincoe. He proudly noted at one point that his 13-year-old daughter was as tall as he was.

Blincoe's memoir took on a life of its own. It went through several editions and parts of it were reprinted whenever a publisher jumped on the factory reform bandwagon. Blincoe was a private man, with a good life for which he had worked very, very hard. He was also a household name. Because of the memoirs, Blincoe was thrown into the company of some very accomplished men. One of them was Francis Bisset Hawkins, a medical doctor. In 1833, Hawkins was actively researching factory conditions for child labourers. Blincoe was one of the men

Hawkins interviewed on his way to recommending a reduction in the hours children could be required to work in factories. Blincoe spoke not only about his own horrific experiences, but also named various colleagues who had been killed or badly injured. He had not forgotten Mary Richards, who had been permanently injured at Lowdham. He also spoke of a man he had known in Stalybridge who had been killed by spinning machines.

Hawkins naturally asked Blincoe about his own children. Did they work in a factory? Blincoe minced no words. He would rather see his children transported than work under the same conditions he had to work under. Here, Blincoe rose to eloquence. There were multiple cruelties in the factory: the air pollution, the risk of deformity from standing long hours, the industrial accidents, children falling asleep because they lacked the stamina to keep going for so many hours. He even hinted that factories could corrupt a child's morals. Most damningly, Blincoe affirmed that the mill owners knew all about the conditions in their mills, right down to the pointless beatings and torture.[18]

Factory reform did not come down to Blincoe's testimony alone, but the memoirs and Blincoe's sworn affidavits were an important part of the improvements that occurred in the lives of factory workers over the next hundred years.

It would be so lovely to report that Blincoe lived well into his nineties and died surrounded by twenty or so grandchildren. Unfortunately, that poetic justice was not forthcoming. He made it into his late sixties and died of bronchitis in the home of his daughter.

Chapter 3

The Artful Dodger and Child Criminals

I n 1968, the musical *Oliver!* delighted audiences with a scene in which the criminal mastermind Fagin sings, 'In this life, one thing counts; in the bank, large amounts. I'm afraid these don't grow on trees. You've got to pick a pocket or two.'

With all the angelic beauty of a boys' choir, Fagin's team of thieves sing the chorus: 'You've got to pick a pocket or two!'

It is a sugary fantasy of a Victorian reality: the underworld of child criminals. When writing the music to *Oliver!*, composer Lionel Bart tapped into Charles Dickens's portrayal of a criminal gang, headed by the adult Fagin, and embodied by the Artful Dodger, whose given name was Jack Dawkins.

Dawkins, aka the Dodger, has become the premier symbol of an elegant, witty thief, someone who seems to 'dodge' all the struggles of a poor child's life: physical abuse, hunger, homelessness, and rough sleeping. The Dodger represents potentially thousands of children in Victorian England's urban areas who lived by crime and begging. 'Between 1801 and 1836 at the Old Bailey alone 103 children received capital sentences,' writes Victorianist Jeannie Duckworth.[1] Fortunately, all those hangings were commuted to prison sentences or deportation. Still, that was just one prison in England, and those were the most serious prosecutions.

Within this shadow world of undocumented children and teenagers, pickpockets were the elite. They were the iceberg tip of child crime. They were the Elon Musks, the Mark Zuckerbergs of the criminal juvenile universe. Some of them had actual schooling in pickpocketing. The fictional Fagin had a real-life equivalent: Issac Solomon. Solomon, who went by the nickname 'Ikey', functioned much as Fagin did.

He supervised a band of child criminals, gave them orders, took a percentage of their earnings, housed them, and gave them a parental figure who was, in most cases, no worse than the biological parent who had thrown them on the streets. Testimony surrounding Solomon attested that he 'trained' children for pickpocketing.

About such 'schools', there is little but anecdotal testimony. Henry Mayhew, author of *London Labour and the London Poor*, is perhaps the only journalist to provide an eyewitness account of this practice. He wrote that 'a coat is suspended from a wall with a bell attached to it and the boy attempts to take a handkerchief from the pocket without the bell ringing. Until he can do this with proficiency, he is not considered well trained.'[2]

Mayhew goes on to describe a more entertaining learning method. The trainer shoves a handkerchief in his coattail and walks up and down the room while his 'trainees' attempt to extract the cloth. This was basic training, however. Advanced learning involved cutting out a pocket with a knife without alerting the pocket's owner. Specialists in picking ladies' pockets were called 'tookers'.[3]

Mayhew claimed to know of at least three such schools and three such teachers operating at that time, 'one of them a young man at Whitechapel, another a young woman at Clerkenwell and a third a middle-aged man residing about Lambeth Walk.'[4] A child as young as 5 might start his training in the Dodger's art.

Pickpockets could work alone, but it was safer to work as a team. Using a well-devised system, one boy performed the actual theft, handed off the goods to a second boy, and that boy would pass the stolen item to a third child. All three of them would run in different directions. It would be difficult to prove that a child was a pickpocket if he were not caught with the goods on him. By tag teaming, the boy with the greatest picking talent would spread out his risk.

It is impossible to know how many child pickpockets lived and thrived in Victoria's England. They were the unnamed, the unknowable. A lack of identity was integral to their survival. The only statistics we have on them are the prison and emigration records of the period. It seems likely that most of them, eventually, were caught. But we can't know that. We know only about the ones who were caught.

The typical child pickpocket was, firstly, a child, with no plan and no real cognitive ability to make a plan or even visualise a future. He would hock his stolen goods quickly. For a culture that abhorred crime, there were a surprising number of places where pickpockets could convert snuff boxes, watches, handkerchiefs, and jewellery into cash. Pawnbrokers were the obvious destination for five-finger discounted merchandise. Hairdressers, tailors, and coffee house employees frequently enough doubled as fences. Even low-end theatres and road houses got in on the criminal action.[5] But lodging houses were particularly reliable as fences. And convenient, because the typical child pickpocket would spend all his money quickly, on food, alcoholic beverages, housing, and, depending on the child's eccentric character, cigars. At a Victorian lodging house, sometimes unfavourably called a 'flophouse' or a 'doss house', the successful pickpocket could convert his ill-gotten goods and immediately spend all or some of them without leaving the premises.

These children frequently took on live-in girlfriends at shockingly young ages. The girl consorts were often prostitutes. In 1852, the Select Committee on Criminal and Destitute Juveniles gathered testimony that many children as young as 12 had already contracted venereal disease.

It is perhaps difficult for the twenty-first century reader to imagine walking into a pub and seeing a 12-year-old sitting at a table unescorted by guardians, with a bottle of Scotch and the remnants of a fine (or at least a big) meal, perhaps accompanied by his 13-year-old mistress. But such a sight would not be unusual in Victorian London, Manchester, or Liverpool.

Child pickpockets and teenage pickpockets were not fools. We know from anecdotal evidence that the cleverest among them changed locations frequently and also gave fake names to law enforcement when they were caught. A repeat offender was much more likely to be transported to Australia, but the court system had no good method in place for logging repetitions. If a lad were brought up on charges in London, then, a few months later, brought up on charges in Manchester under a different name, the Victorian administration was largely helpless about putting his criminal record together in one file. Admittedly, the capacity to track criminals improved in the 1860s with more formal parish record keeping. It helped when parishes were required to record every new birth and the name of the baby. But forensics and DNA sampling were far, far off. A truly clever and seasoned criminal could pass for a first-time criminal rather easily.

And it was worth doctoring one's record because the Victorian attitude toward repeat offenders cannot be described as 'boys will be boys'. Dublin magistrate J. Shaw sentenced an average of 350 children a year. This is how he dealt with the repeats: 'I generally give them, for the first offence, three months; for the second six months; and if it is a young boy I do not transport him but give him twelve months imprisonment for the third offence.'[6] Shaw's tone here is troubling in that it suggests he sees himself as a paragon of fairness and liberality. He goes on to explain that he has sentenced children under the age of 15 to forced emigration when they are particularly 'hardened'.

At the same time that he was handing out these sentences, Shaw also clearly saw that the 'greater part are destitute and abandoned children, or the offspring of profligate parents'. Shaw betrays a glaring lack of self-awareness when he declares that, when a convict has nice parents, such as 'small tradesmen', he lets the boy go, trusting his parents will bring him around.[7] Under Shaw's regime, the advantaged got more advantages, and the disadvantaged got prison sentences and deportation.

Child criminals were not, universally, unable to save money. Some of them would save enough to buy fine clothes. Dressed as gentlemen, they would not be out of place in finer neighbourhoods. They would have access to the track, the train station, and the shopping centres. There, purloined handkerchiefs and watches would be more valuable, the wallets fuller. The pickpocket could amass wealth.

If one sets aside the imminent danger of being imprisoned, very possibly hanged, or transported, some pickpockets did well financially. According to W. A. Miles of the Prison Discipline Society, summers were the pickpocket's 'season'. During peak activity, the best thieves could walk back to the lodging house with £1 a day.[8] That pound, amassed in 1839, would be roughly equivalent to £80 today.

This information makes it possible to fantasise about a child who saves enough money to retire from thievery and set up as a respectable citizen, much as does the imaginary main character in Thomas Hardy's *Mayor of Casterbridge*.

Let us, for a lovely moment, explore how that might have worked. The really successful pickpockets would hone their craft, they would spot opportunity, they would manage risk, they would evade capture. The smartest would work for themselves, minimise social contacts, and, most importantly, they would retire as soon as they had enough money to do something legitimate.

But here the fantasy stumbles. How would a boy like the Dodger transition into civilian life? The obvious answer was to set up shop as a tailor or in another high-end trade, but, having spent his childhood learning to pick pockets, he would not have the training to be a tailor. And Victorian society had no room for latecomers to a respectable trade.

Nor would a pickpocket be temperamentally suited to the boring work that non-criminals, with normal levels of adrenaline, don't mind doing. Grooming horses, cutting meat, bailing hay. These occupations would be stultifyingly dull for someone who was used to the high of pulling a watch or wallet out of the back pocket of a mark, not just once but up to several times a day.

It is not entirely impossible that a few successful child criminals integrated themselves into semi-respectable societies, but unlikely. In point of unromantic fact, most of them would have ended up like the Dodger – on a ship to Australia.

As a representative of the Victorian pickpocket, the Artful Dodger remains an icon of wit, dexterity, and evasion. Readers like him for many reasons, but mostly because he floats above the world of hard work and struggle that most of us accept as our lot. People like the Dodger for the reasons that they liked Bonnie and Clyde, Dillinger, and Jesse James. These outlaws provide an outlet for our longings for escape and rebellion, our yearnings to give the finger to the law and all the oppressive trappings of civilised order.

Lamentably, the Dodger was not a typical child criminal of the Victorian era. He was the pinnacle of the criminal food chain. We know this because of the pecking order that existed in Victorian prisons. The most respected prisoners, the aristocrats of the Old Bailey, were the pickpockets and house breakers. In 1839, W. A. Miles wrote: 'Pickpockets and house breakers ... looked down on mere shoplifters, who, in their turn, were superior to sneak thieves.'[9]

The Rookeries

The lives of most child criminals were much less glamorous. Their lives were not just unpoetical, they were sordid. Most of these children, like the Dodger, did report back to an adult at the end of the day. But, in most cases, the adult mastermind behind the child was simply a terrible mother or father.

These parents were not necessarily criminals by nature. Many of them were alcoholics and drug addicts. Others were newcomers to the city who had been displaced by the industrial revolution and enclosure of common rural spaces. In many cases, these parents came to London, Birmingham, Manchester, or Liverpool sincerely hoping to find work. But so many people had the same idea, and jobs became increasingly hard to come by, especially for people with no skills but those related to agriculture.

The poorest children in London lived in 'rookeries'. These were dark alleys, so crowded, diseased, and dirty that no respectable people dared enter. We know little about these slums because they were almost entirely shunned, even by the journalists and reformers whose responsibility it was to report on circumstances and effect positive change. Even the police dropped their investigations at the outer edge of these rookeries.

London newspaper reporter Charles Knight, magistrate Gilbert Abbott A'Becket, writer William Beaver Neale, and reformer Henry Mayhew were among the very few people who braved the rookeries to report on them. In 1841, Knight visited the St Giles rookery and reported that the buildings were so old, it was a wonder they were still standing. The gutters were stagnant, and the undisposed garbage sat in piles. Knight saw groups of women all dressed in rags, men with nothing to do. This vast no man's land of London was a residential ghetto where even business cared not to venture. The only two businesses he saw were a vendor of stale vegetables and a rag shop. Yet, somehow, many of the residents were inebriated, drink being the only real anodyne to the worst poverty. The rookery was so crowded that, at night, the residents jockeyed to find enough space to recline. Knight speculated that the 'animal heat' of so many bodies crammed together was enough to heat the rooms in the absence of any fuel.

He went on to say there was no privacy anywhere. Every apartment was accessible by every other. The door frames were rotten, and the doors coming off their hinges. The accommodations offered 'the last and frailest shelter that can be interposed between man and the elements'.[10]

The rookeries were not specifically designed to breed child criminals, but the creation of such children was inevitable, given the poverty of the people who lived in these slums, combined with the lack of education for children of poor families. Abbott A'Becket bravely combed the rookeries of Norfolk, Suffolk, Essex, and Reading. In those slums, he found 'a class of unfortunate children likely to prove a fertile source of crime'.[11] He noted that these children were often conceived due to overcrowding, lack of privacy, and the profound temptation to anaesthetise the pain of poverty with casual sex and alcohol. On a related note, Henry Mayhew wrote that the daughters of poor families were much more likely to become prostitutes than the daughters of the rich or middle class.

William Beaver Neale did a systematic study of juvenile delinquency in Manchester in which he bravely identified poverty as the root cause of child criminality. Vast stretches of Manchester, including Angel Meadow, New Town, Little Ireland, Pop Gardens, Gaythorn, Knott Mill, and Deansgate had become criminal slums.[12] Unsurprisingly, crime paid very little in Manchester, and the most immoral inhabitants of that city occupied, by far, the worst dwellings: 'Here, then, the narrow, ill-ventilated, and filthy streets, with their stunted and dirty hovels, markedly contrast with ... the public buildings situated in the more airy and commodious quarters of the town.' Neale went on to write that dwellings in the Manchester slums were not just crowded, they were characterised by 'confinement, darkness, nakedness, and filth'.[13]

How, one might reasonably ask, did such rookeries come into existence, and why did the government do nothing to stop them from developing? And the answer is: a combination of unchecked capitalism combined with subdivision gone mad. The slums of London and Manchester might look like no man's lands, but they, in fact, had owners and landlords. Many, many landlords.

According to London historian Peter Ackroyd, the London area of Church Lane was majority owned by eight people. These landowners kept themselves at a distance from their own rookeries by renting out whole streets to more hands-on landlords who then, in turn, subdivided the street and rented out the individual houses. The leaseholders on the houses rented out rooms. And then the madness started, in earnest, with room holders renting out space in their rooms to multiple families at one time. 'It represents an absolute hierarchy of need, or desperation, in which no one assumed responsibility for the dreadful conditions which prevailed,' writes Ackroyd.[14] The hyper subdivision, the reckless disregard for the dangers of rape, robbery, and contagion – all quite legal.

Within these rookeries, desperate parents cast their offspring on the street to find their own food. Parents of daughters often directly or indirectly sold their children into prostitution. Boys would be sent into the city and told to come home with money or valuables. How the child got the valuables did not matter to such parents. Some children succeeded as beggars, though begging could also be prosecuted as a crime. Other children had to steal.

And the vast majority of 'thefts' were petty. The reason we know that so many children were criminals is that they were arrested for the smallest crimes – stealing a piece of fruit, a loaf of bread, a pin, a sheaf of paper, a handful of coals. There was almost nothing related to daily survival so humble that a street urchin did not want it. These street children would steal the clothes that were hanging on a line at the back of someone's tenement.

The icon of Victorian child thievery is a ragamuffin lifting a handkerchief out of a rich man's pocket. That rich man will never miss it. This is, in so many ways, a deceptive image.

The reality was much worse. The main marks of urban child thieves were other struggling poor people. Street stalls made the easiest targets. They were out in the open, no security, typically only one stall employee who could not leave his or her merchandise to chase someone who had just lifted an orange or a loaf. The individual thefts might not have been great. But, for the person who owned the stall, that loaf or orange might have been the day's profit margin. And if such a stall was a frequent target of multiple thieves, the merchant could go out of business.

By today's standards, it might seem outrageous that a child would be sent to prison for stealing a piece of fruit. But in 1851 and 1852, fifty-five children under the age of 14 were sent to a correctional institute for fruit stealing and similar offences, in which the stolen item was worth less than sixpence. During the same period, another forty-eight children were sentenced for stealing items worth less than a shilling.[15]

Small retail businesses were also fairly easy targets. Child criminals had multiple methods for robbing such establishments, and they often tag teamed. In some cases, a band of children would create a ruckus on the street outside a store. When the owner of the store came out to investigate, one of the children would pop inside and rob the register. A more elaborate ruse was to throw a cap into a store, go in to collect it, then rob the register while the owner was busy in some other area of his store. If caught with a hand in the till, the boy would claim he only came in to retrieve the cap which his friends had thrown in as a prank.[16]

Punishments that Did Not Fit the Crime

One feels for the small business owners who had to absorb losses incurred by desperate children. But the greater share of our sympathy still has to go to the children. The punishments dispensed would be condemned by any civilised country today as human rights violations. At one point, a judge condemned a 10-year-old boy to hanging for a petty theft. The judge's reasoning was that to let the boy off would be to encourage such crime. In 1801, a 13-year-old boy was hanged for unlawfully entering a home and stealing a spoon. In 1808, a girl of 11 and her 8-year-old sister were hanged. Hanging children would not be outlawed until the Children's Act of 1908 made it illegal to execute someone under 16.

Just because a child was not hanged did not mean he could survive the rigours of prison or the extra deprivations he could be subjected to if he failed to be a model prisoner. James Richmond was only 10 years old and serving a sentence in the Millbank prison when he died of starvation. He was repeatedly put on a bread-and-water-only diet and even deprived of a mattress to sleep on. An investigation into his death found that the deprivations he suffered were the sole cause of death.[17]

Such sentences were notable during the Victorian period, but not an anomaly. In the eighteenth and nineteenth centuries, the legal age of responsibility in Britain was 7. That meant that 7-year-olds and up were effectively tried as adults. British law did, theoretically, recognise the principle of doli incapax (which literally means 'incapable of crime'), which asks whether a child understands the difference between right and wrong. Under British law of the Victorian age, prosecutors were supposed to prove that a child criminal under 14 understood the criminal nature of what he was doing. But, in practice, most tweens brought up on charges were assumed to know right from wrong, and no real doli incapax test was administered or considered. The fact that a child had committed a crime was considered proof that he or she knew what crime was.

In the course of her investigations, human rights activist Mary Carpenter discovered many imprisoned children for whom the doli incapax principal had been completely ignored. Seven- and 8-year-olds in the Millbank Penitentiary had no clue why they were serving time. An 11-year-old girl serving a year's sentence for stealing a sovereign could not tell the difference between a sovereign and a shilling.

Children sentenced to prison were not always segregated from adult criminals. In particular, child criminals awaiting trial usually resided with the grown-ups. It was well understood that this kind of mixing could serve as a criminal education for a child. The Select Committee on Criminal Convictions noted in 1828 that the system of mixing child and adult criminals was inevitably corrupting to the child:

> The boy is committed to prison for trial; the degradation and the company he meets there prepares his mind for every vice; after a long delay he is sentenced to six months or a year's imprisonment, he herds with felons and comes out an accomplished thief, detesting the laws of the country and prepared with means to avoid them.[18]

Much more common as a means of punishing and 'teaching' children were the severe beatings. The most common tool used in these legitimised assaults was the birch rod, but children's backs also felt the bite of the cat o' nine tails, a whip with multiple cotton straps, referred to casually as the 'cat'. The nine whip strands were knotted to make contact with the offender's back even more damaging. The cat was designed to inflict the greatest possible pain in proportion to the exertion of the whipper. Where a simple whip would leave one welt or gash, the cat could leave as many as nine at one time.

Cat whipping was controversial in the nineteenth century, with some humanitarians ardently opposing it. But the lethality of such a punishment was not fully demonstrated until 1846 when a British Army private died as a direct result of a cat o' nine tails whipping. The private's name was Frederick John White. He ran afoul of military discipline when he got drunk and argued with a superior. At some point during this conflict, White touched (not assaulted) the superior with a metal rod. For this, he was sentenced to 150 cat o' nine tails lashes.

He needed immediate hospitalisation after this sentence was served, and it looked for a while like he might survive. But after a few days, he died and a spate of autopsies finally concluded that the whipping killed him.[19] This investigation resulted, not in the outlawing of the cat, but in a mandate that no whipping should go on for more than fifty lashes.

Sentences stipulated a certain number of lashes. Keeping in mind that 150 lashes were lethal to an adult male helps us put into context the use of a potentially murderous weapon on minors. The Bristol House of Correction, in particular, liked to whip its offenders, including children, with the cat.

Still, a child or teenager might prefer being whipped given the alternatives that existed. Children who ran afoul of Victorian law were sentenced to hard labour which could consist of stone crushing or riverbank cleaning. When no such real work was available, 'hard labour' could amount to simple torture. Prisons forced inmates onto treadwheels, giant cylinders which could be turned by multiple prisoners who marched up an automated staircase. The treadwheel, also known as the everlasting staircase, was designed by William Cubitt in 1818, and up to forty prisoners could work it at one time. These wheels could be used to grind corn or pump water. But when no such materials were available, prisoners could be forced onto a wheel that produced nothing, just to torture them. This kind of 'hard labour' could be administered to adult and child criminals alike for up to two full weeks. It was not until 1843 that the Prison Inspectors' General

Survey recommended that children under 14 be exempted from the treadwheel on the grounds that it could harm their health.

The Leicester Gaol crank was a similar make-work torture device. Instead of stepping on an endless moving staircase, prisoners cranked a wheel around in circles, using their hands, in order to shift a set of paddles inside a drum full of sand. Sentences stipulated a number of rotations during a six-hour shift. A child sentenced to this hardship might be required to do 6,000–14,000 revolutions per day. Food and water could be withheld from prisoners who did not complete their quota of rotations. Prison staff could, at their discretion, tighten or loosen the crank, making it harder or easier to rotate. Some people believe this is the origin of the slang word, 'screw', as applied to a prison guard.

If a prisoner refused to 'crank', he could be put in a straitjacket and then suspended from a hook in the wall. Edward Andrews, a 15-year-old prisoner at the Birmingham Borough Gaol, frequently ended up suspended in space in his straitjacket. Andrews was a typical Victorian child criminal. In 1853, he was serving his third prison sentence. On this occasion, he had stolen 4 pounds of meat. When he was only 13, he had served time for stealing fruit out of someone's garden. At 14, he had been arrested again, this time for throwing stones. On more than one occasion, Andrews deliberately broke the crank he was assigned to. Like Bartleby the Scrivener, he simply preferred not to. The day prior to his death, he was still trying to escape prison, as evidenced by his breaking a bar on his cell window.

For a persistent offender, Andrews was remarkably well mannered. He was never violent in deed or word, though he was known to cuss to his fellow prisoners. He did not even complain when being subjected to the crank and the straitjacket. When he refused to crank, he was put on a starvation diet of bread and water. Despite the malnutrition, Andrews was in perfect health when he hanged himself in his cell. His suicide was the subject of a substantial Royal Commission investigation, reported in the liberal leaning *Birmingham Journal*. This investigation found Andrews had been subjected to punishment that was both cruel and illegal. Yet, with flagrant inconsistency, the commission refused to prosecute anyone, calling the incident 'unfortunate'. The Birmingham Prison and others continued making prisoners turn the crank.[20]

The most important thing to remember about child criminality and imprisonment in the Victorian era is how seldom the punishment fit the crime. Today, a 12-year-old shoplifter would most likely be sent home to his parents with a warning. At worst, he might get slapped with a CBO (Criminal Behaviour Order). In 1837, the same shoplifter might well end up in Coldbath Fields prison. In that year, Coldbath Fields held 358 children under the age of 13. And the vast majority of them, 276, were in for 'simple larceny', also known as petty theft. Two of these children had been imprisoned for stealing larger amounts still under the value of £5. Twenty had committed larceny 'from the person'. In other words, they had been caught picking pockets. Thirteen of the 12-and-under prisoners had been servants who stole small amounts from their employers. By contrast, very, very few children were in prison for violent or what we, today, would identify as serious crimes. There was one child convicted of murder, another of assault, yet another of arson, and three for stealing horses. In 1837, Coldbath Fields held more convicts under the age of 13 than over that age.[21]

The Hulks and Parkhurst

In *Oliver Twist*, the Artful Dodger 'dodges' consequences right up to tale's end, when he is arrested for the petty theft of a snuff box and a few pastries. The last time the reader sees the Dodger, he is headed to Australia, under a deportation order, to expiate his crimes in the new world. Optimists will assume that Jack, like his literary precedents Colonel Jack and Moll Flanders, will find success and respectability in the new world. Maybe the Dodger will marry and produce a fleet of offspring. Despite Dickens's profligacy with the written word, he never gives the reader closure on the Artful Dodger's future destiny. The reader is left to hope that the Dodger will continue to float above the sordid circumstances of a world which can be so cruel to children.

In sending the Artful Dodger to the colonies, Dickens again captured a trend of his age. Britain had colonies, and those colonies were hungry for cheap labour. Therefore, anyone and everyone who didn't fit the social norms at home could end up on a ship bound for elsewhere. Prior to 1776, and the United States' war for independence, prisoners had been sent en masse to the colonies in America. By the Victorian era, that avenue of immigration for British prisoners had mostly closed, and the undesirables, which included so many, many children, were mostly deported to Australia, Tasmania, or New Zealand.

Indeed, if a society deems it necessary to isolate and punish children who steal small sums of money and items of little value, and if those children become half the prisoners you intend to lock up, then a solution must be found to deal with all those young criminals. The British came up with the idea of sending these kids overseas.

It was rarely possible to send a child directly from court to another country, however. So prison institutions were set up as holding facilities to imprison children slated for forced emigration. Unfortunately, there were so many prisoners that the existing prisons could not accommodate them. To accommodate the overflow of prisoners, including children guilty of petty theft, prison hulks were deployed. The prison hulks were decommissioned ships, deemed no longer seaworthy. To ensure that the prisoners did not restore them to seaworthiness, their rudders, masts, and sails were stripped off. Parliament authorised the use of hulks as prisoner accommodation in 1776, when the US War of Independence cut off the previously convenient practice of sending convicts to America. The use of hulks was meant to be a two-year emergency measure. That emergency continued for eighty years.

The hulks were mostly moored in river harbours, and the prisoners set to the hard labour of cleaning riverbanks. In 1823, child prisoners, all of them 14 and younger, were placed in the *Bellerophon*, and the noble ship's name was changed to *Captivity*. The *Bellerophon* was a proud vessel that had been deployed in war against the French, served in the Battle of Trafalgar, then used to transport Napoleon to Plymouth harbour.

The *Captivity* only served as a prison hulk for two years. Children quartered there were transferred to the smaller HMS *Euryalus* which was forced to accommodate 383 kids. It was impossible to control the boys. Even though the ship could not be sailed, the tweens mutinied regularly. The older boys bullied the younger, smaller ones. Dietary deficiencies led to rampant scurvy. The ship chaplain used religion as a weapon against the juvenile delinquents in his charge. If they so much as whispered during one of his sermons, he sentenced them to an eighteen-lash whipping with a cat o' nine tails.[22] A medical practitioner named Thomas Dexter treated the illness and injuries of many boys on the *Euryalus*. Dexter himself had been a prisoner on one of the hulks and gave testimony against the *Euryalus* in 1835: 'I have seen it in a newspaper that a Judge has sentenced a boy out of mercy to him to the hulks, I have made the observation that was it a child of mine I would rather see him dead at my feet than see him sent to that place.'[23]

Dexter went on to say that the youngest hulk prisoner he had treated was a boy aged 6. The boy had been convicted for robbery in Birmingham. The surprisingly compassionate judge asked the child's mother if she would take him in, should the judge pass a lenient sentence. The boy's mother said she would not, so the judge thought the best course of action was forced emigration, which was how the child ended up on a prison hulk. He died in Dexter's hospital shortly after admission.

Malnutrition can have many consequences, including scurvy. Scurvy is caused by a lack of vitamin C which, in its latest stages, causes one's teeth to fall out. Prior to the twentieth century, scurvy was a constant menace on ships because it was difficult to keep food fresh, and fresh food, especially fruits and vegetables, are essential to maintaining healthy doses of vitamin C. We can certainly understand that men at a ten days' ocean distance from any markets could develop health problems from their diet.

What is more difficult to understand is how children housed in a stationary ship used as a prison were getting scurvy. But when we look at the children's daily schedule, it becomes clear: they skipped tea and supper. In 1828, a select committee made a report on the *Euryalus* that showed the boys being rousted from sleep at 5.30 am, at which time they ate breakfast, then swabbed all three decks. At 6.45 am, they were set to work making clothing. At noon, they ate 'dinner'. They were locked in their wards and supervised by guards during this meal. Afterwards they did laps in the open air. During a brief free time, they were not allowed to play. The prisoners then went back to making clothing until 5.45 pm, after which they had one hour of education, followed by prayers. Then they were locked up in their wards for the night. From this report, it appears that the noon meal was the last food the children had before 5.30 am rolled around again.[24]

If the Victorian disposal of its child criminals teaches us anything, it teaches that deprivation does not lead to penitence or reform. It leads, instead, to bullying and recidivism. That was certainly the case with the *Euryalus*. Everyone who investigated the hulks and everyone who heard testimony about them knew they were bad. It should have come as no surprise to anyone that eight out of ten children who served time on the *Euryalus* returned to a life of crime upon being freed. However, despite investigations that revealed terrible abuses and results, child criminals continued to serve time on hulks through the mid-1850s.

Parkhurst, a prison for boys only, was another way station for child criminals awaiting transportation. It was positioned on the Isle of Wight. In 1838, the prison received its first shipment of children and by the end of the year, there were 146 child inmates. Parkhurst was a soft landing for a boy criminal. This new, somewhat experimental prison was, effectively, a transition centre in which children demonstrated their readiness to make a contribution in the new world. It was worth it for a boy to endure the Bible reading, the lectures, the criticism because, at the end of his Parkhurst prison sentence, lay possible freedom in Australia.

There were children who were 'incorrigible', i.e. too difficult for the gentler leadership of Parkhurst to handle. Prison records document one boy, John Gavin, who was sent to Australia at the age of 13 when whipping and other punishments did not make him compliant enough for the Parkhurst culture. He had been imprisoned for larceny, but by the time he got to Australia, he was a hardened enough criminal. He made it only two years in the new world before being executed for murder.

By Victorian standards, however, Parkhurst was an experiment in liberal enlightenment. Children under the age of 13 received one and a half days of education a week. This education was heavy on the Bible, but there was some reading, maths, and 'writing', which meant copying words from a book onto paper. There was also some geography and, strangely enough, music during these short interludes in the classroom. A percentage of boys under 13 were taught to be tailors. Others got stuck pumping water or farming the eighty-five Isle of Wight acres owned by the prison. As Australia mostly needed farmers and farm hands, this was not the worst training the lads could receive.

If a boy turned 13 in Parkhurst, or if he entered Parkhurst at the age of 13 or higher, and if his behaviour had been compliant enough, he might be taught a valuable skill: brick making, brick laying, blacksmithing, painting, carpentry, baking, or shoe making. If his luck were not in ascendance, a young teenager would get sent to the kitchen, laundry, or garden to learn what there was to learn there. The boys all learned knitting which meant they could supply their own socks.

The boys at Parkhurst did not starve, though those sent to the Refractory Ward for misbehaviour were put on reduced rations. In general, they ate a great deal of bread, cocoa, molasses, soup, potatoes, and at least a few times a week, boiled beef. As time wore on, plum pudding was trotted out on Sundays as an inducement to good behaviour. Children who had offended the wardens that week did not get any.

Historians know little about what happened to the boys of Parkhurst, except that the prison did fulfil its mission of sending dozens of children to the new world. From 1845 to 1852, boats full of boys sailed from Great Britain to Australia and Tasmania. Some of these children were pardoned and became free citizens of the new world. We know little else. They are mostly lost to history.

The Emigrants

There are many rags-to-riches and vice-to-virtue stories among the Australian immigrant convicts of the nineteenth century. John Rowland Jones was convicted of embezzlement, but in Australia, he went legit, becoming first a newspaper reporter and, eventually, an editor. The architect Francis Howard Greenway was convicted of forgery. In New South Wales, he became the first government architect, and designed many now famous buildings, including at least two churches. Alfred Chopin was wrongfully convicted of receiving stolen goods and transported to Australia. His life took an upswing, however, when he became a popular portrait photographer. He photographed many famous Australians, and some of his work has been preserved for posterity. What these people have in common is that they were adults when convicted and adults when transported.

The odds are always stacked harder and taller against a child whose entire life has been one long round of poverty, abuse, deprivation, ignorance, desperation, and finally forced emigration, often for a trivial offence. The chequered career of John Hudson is, one fears, representative of what became of children sent to Australia. Hudson was either orphaned or abandoned, but never made it to a foundling hospital which might have cared for him until he was 15. He became a chimney sweep and, by the age of 9, he had been convicted for theft of items worth more than 2 shillings and slated for transport. He was first slated for forced emigration to the United States, but there was a mutiny aboard the *Mercury* on which he sailed. The ship went off course. The escaped convicts were rounded back up and Hudson was interned in a hulk prison, the decommissioned *Dunkirk*, for three years.

Hudson's claim to fame is that he was the youngest child to sail with the celebrated first fleet, a flotilla of eleven ships that carried the first Europeans and Africans to Australia in 1787. Hudson was 13 when he arrived, alive, at Sydney Cove. The brave new world that Hudson inherited was in the throes of a food shortage. We know nothing of his first two years in Australia, but in 1790, he was transferred to Norfolk

Island. The ship on which he travelled, the HMS *Sirius*, was wrecked, and the transported food stores lost at sea. The convicts, along with the marines who had sailed with them, were left to scramble for food. The next thing we know about Hudson is that he received fifty lashes for violating curfew, meaning he was outdoors after 9.00 pm.[25] That is the last record we have of this child. Like other child criminals of the Victorian age, he disappears into the annals of history. His beginnings were unpropitious, his immigration a disaster, and one assumes that he did not achieve the same respectability and success that Greenway, Chopin, and Rowland Jones attained.

Of course, there is always an exception to every rule, and Mary Wade is an important exception. Mary Wade was a beggar and street sweeper until, at the age of either 12 or 14, she confronted another girl and stole her dress, cap, and tippet. She unloaded the dress at a pawnbroker, but was caught and arrested with the tippet still in her possession. She was tried at the Old Bailey and sentenced to be hanged.

And there her story would have ended, but for a celebration taking place at the opposite end of English society. Early in 1789, King George III was enjoying one of his frequent respites from chronic mental illness. England breathed a communal sigh of relief so deep and grateful that all the women on death row, on which Mary sat, had their sentences commuted to transportation. Instead of being hanged from the neck until dead, Mary sailed aboard the *Lady Juliana*, the first convict ship to bring only women and children to Australia.

In Australia, Mary unveiled her great and heretofore hidden talent – an almost supernatural fertility. The *Lady Juliana* delivered her to Norfolk Island, and in that volcanic wasteland, she had three children. While living in a tent in Sydney, she had two more. She lived with Jonathan Brooker beginning in 1809, and a mere eight years later, they were married. Both Brooker and Wade obtained certificates of freedom, and she had twenty-one more children. A bushfire in 1823 financially devastated the Brooker family, but they recovered, and by 1828 they owned over sixty acres of land. Mary lived to the ripe age of 84, long enough for her descendants to number 300. Tens of thousands of Australians carry her DNA, including former Prime Minister Kevin Rudd. Mary Wade is, literally, the mother of her people.

Readers of *Oliver Twist* hope and pray that the Dodger met with an equally pleasant fate.

Chapter 4

The Nancies: Child Sex Workers

The subject of child prostitution is so horrible that most contemporary readers would probably like to think about something else. The Victorians were no different. They not only wished to ignore child trafficking, they wished to cover it up. The great Anthony Ashley Cooper, 7th Earl of Shaftesbury, spent his life in social reform, rescuing children from the mines and the chimneys. But even he had no stomach for confronting the underworld of the child sex trade. When asked to do something, he said he wished to know even less about the subject than he already did.[1]

In considering the real-life Oliver Twists, one might similarly wish to forget Nancy, perhaps the novel's most pitiful character. Nancy is the 17-year-old who was murdered by her boyfriend at the end of a short life characterised by abuse, moral corruption, thievery, and prostitution. And there is little comfort to be taken in knowing that she was just a fictional character. She was emblematic of thousands of children and teens who became Victorian prostitutes in real life.

Though there continues to be some debate about the exact character of Nancy's crimes, especially on the amateur internet, Dickens told his readers plainly in the 1846 edition of the novel, 'The boys are pickpockets, and the girl is a prostitute.'[2]

The confusion about Nancy's status as a sex worker comes, in part, from Dickens's unwillingness to be raunchy. He doubted the ability of his readers to tolerate an overt depiction of prostitution. He made a point of modulating the language of all his criminal characters, but it was particularly important that Nancy not get into the details of her work.

No less consulting my own taste, than the manners of the age, I endeavoured, while I painted it in all its fallen and degraded aspect, to banish from the lips of the lowest character I introduced, any expression that could by possibility offend; and rather to lead to the unavoidable inference that its existence was of the most debased and vicious kind, than to prove it elaborately by words and deeds. In the case of the girl, in particular, I kept this intention constantly in view.[3]

In writing *Oliver Twist*, Dickens hoped to expose a system that treated children so unjustly. He was particularly outraged by the way so-called 'fallen' girls were thrown aside by society. In an 1867 edition of the novel, he condemns his fellow Victorians for idolising the sex trade when it is glamorously and expensively packaged, but condemning the lowly street prostitute: 'A Mrs. Massaroni, being a lady in short petticoats and fancy dress, is a thing to imitate in tableaux and have in lithograph in pretty songs; but a Nancy, being a creature in a cotton gown and cheap shawl, is not to be thought of.'[4]

Dickens here hits on an important point relative to prostitution in the Victorian era. It was never respectable, in the fullest sense of the term, but the worst judgement and punishment was held in reserve for the poorest practitioners of that trade: girls whose parents sold them into the sex trade and girls who resorted to selling sex to feed themselves and their illegitimate babies being the most obvious targets of injustice. As Dickens wrote, 'It is wonderful how Virtue turns from dirty stockings; and how Vice, married to ribbons and a little gay attire, changes her name, as wedded ladies do, and becomes Romance.'[5]

He makes an apt point. It was not impossible for a woman to knowingly enter the trade of prostitution, make money, acquire assets, and come to a comfortable truce with polite society, possibly by scrubbing her identity. The most obvious promotion for a savvy street girl was to establish her own brothel. Such was the story of George Bernard Shaw's *Mrs Warren's Profession*, a play about a woman who starts out in the sex trade and ends up running it.

Novelist and poet Thomas Hardy also noted that, of all the dangers that can befall a woman, losing her virginity might not be the worst. His poem 'The Ruined Maid' satirises the idea that a girl making her own money, buying nice clothes, and eating nutritious meals is 'ruined'. The titular 'ruined maid' is a young woman named 'Melia who is spotted in town by an old friend. The friend immediately wants to know why 'Melia now has such nice clothes and looks healthy: 'You left us in tatters, without shoes or socks, / Tired of digging potatoes, and spudding up docks; / And now you've gay bracelets and bright feathers three!' exclaims 'Melia's friend. 'Melia replies: 'Yes: that's how we dress when we're ruined.'

When asked why she has smooth hands and a 'delicate cheek', the former farm girl 'Melia repeats that she is ruined, and: 'We never do work when we're ruined.'

Hardy was right on the money. Prostitution was the most highly paid work a Victorian woman could do. It was risky work. The most immediate dangers were sexually transmitted diseases and pregnancy. Young women who plied this trade were also in danger of being beaten or killed by their clients. But other women, the so-called 'virtuous' working poor, were also at risk of violence from their husbands or strangers. They were at risk of overwork and exhaustion. They were at risk from unhealthy living conditions and poor nutrition. And though their risk of venereal disease was lower than that of a prostitute, they could still contract an STD from a husband, boyfriend, or rapist.

Given the high overall risks of being any Victorian woman not born to wealth, a savvy, unsentimental woman who was brave enough to flout convention, intentionally, and without giving way to shame and self-pity, could live a better, more independent life than her peers who stayed on the farm.

Nancy did not embody those women, though. Nancy was another of Fagin's victims, raised by him since she was 5 years old. Prostitutes like Nancy were most often railroaded into prostitution, frequently at the behest of parents.

Such a child was Jane Cameron. In her startling book, *Fagin's Children*, Jeannie Duckworth relates that Jane was born into a Glasgow ghetto to an unstable mother who took in boarders and drank up what small income she made. She had got into trouble with the police for acting out. When Jane was 5, her mother explained that she must fend for herself during the day, though the child was still allowed to come home at night. This was not an uncommon practice for the poorest families which explains why child gangs were still a thing in late nineteenth-century Britain. Jane begged on the streets and gave whatever money she made to her mother on returning home as if she herself was a lodger and not the woman's biological child.

At 10, Jane found work, as Robert Blincoe had, at a cotton factory. She was paid a starvation wage, but that pittance went to keep her mother in booze. There was no upward mobility for Jane's family. A man who represented himself as Jane's father introduced her to the trade of prostitution. In this life, she met many new people, none of them wholesome. At 11, she formed a relationship with a 14-year-old boy named Ewan, and she became a thief. By 12, she was serving her first prison sentence. As so many junior offenders do, she shared a cell with someone who was able to accelerate her progress toward a life of crime. When she graduated from prison, she moved in with Ewan, who protected himself from the consequences of crime by sending Jane out to steal for them.

She was pregnant during her second prison sentence of sixty days. By the time she was freed, Ewan had taken up with another young woman. Jane delivered her baby with no medical attention, no friends, no family. An older woman from Ireland took her in, and Jane returned to begging, which she did on the streets with her baby in her arms. But her baby soon died of scarlet fever, and Jane once again took up thievery which was, apparently, more lucrative for a child, barely into her teens, who lacked the pathos of a nursing infant. At 15, she was serving yet another prison sentence, in a Glasgow prison.[6]

It seems likely that Nancy's story was similar. Abandoned by parents, she is introduced to a life of crime long before she can develop any sense of right and wrong. Nancy absorbs the full terror of what she has become only as a very young adult. Then, instead of cultivating rage against Fagin and a society that throws away penniless children, she blames herself, telling the virtuous Rose Maylie that the latter need not hesitate to pull away from 'such as she': 'I am the infamous creature you have heard of, that lives among the thieves … Do not mind shrinking openly from me, lady … I am well used to it. The poorest women fall back, as I make my way along the crowded pavement.'[7]

The Nancies were the worst victims of legal prostitution. The younger, poorer, the more unconscious of what she was getting into, and the more unwilling a girl was to enter the trade, the worse her outcomes. Such children generally had no access or limited access to whatever income they 'earned'. They could be thrown on the streets when they got pregnant or diseased. They often served prison sentences. If they were trafficked to another country, they were frequently held prisoner in the establishment that received them.

As dark as Jane Crowley's story is, we must go yet darker. Victorian London harboured not just a thriving industry in child sex work, it also traded in the rape of virgins. Florence Rush explains that this business was so brisk, there was a known pay scale, depending on the 'quality' of the virgin:

> There were never enough 'voluntary prostitutes' to meet the voracious Victorian demand. Consequently, enterprising entrepreneurs established a system of obtaining 'involuntary prostitutes'. Men who wanted sex with little girls were prepared to pay a good price, and a standard pricing system brought about twenty pounds for a healthy working-class girl between the ages of fourteen and eighteen, a hundred pounds for a middle-class girl of the same age; and as much as four hundred pounds for a child from the upper class under age twelve…[8]

Experts who can stand to write about it agree that defloration mania began in the eighteenth century and continued through the nineteenth.

This subculture was virtually impossible to monitor or prosecute because the men who enjoyed raping children had no shame or remorse. They had everything to gain by keeping it hidden. Meanwhile, the men and women who had the moral courage to bust it feared losing their reputations by associating with such a sordid enterprise. At the end of the day, almost everything we know about child prostitution comes from journalists who risked their respectability to enter brothels and talk to people who trafficked children. Most primary testimony concerning the Victorian child sex trade comes from two very brave reforming writers, William Thomas Stead and Alfred Stace Dyer.

English Girls Trafficked to Belgium

Dyer exposed a sex trafficking route between rural England and Brussels, Belgium in his first-person account, *The European Slave Trade in English Girls*. He starts this book by observing that the sex trade in continental Europe is heavily regulated by the government. This regulation means that the brothels operate in the open. However, this disclosure of purposes does not exist to protect the young women who actually provide the service. It protects their customers and agents. The girls themselves, Dyer notes, are effectively prisoners:

> From the day they enter these houses, they are not allowed to wear their own clothing, but are forced to wear garments of a disgusting nature, for the hire of which, and also for everything they require, they are charged exorbitant prices. They are thus kept deeply in debt and terrified with the threat of imprisonment if they dare to attempt to leave without paying.[9]

Dyer goes on to report that laws prohibit underage girls from serving as prostitutes; to get around that point of law, girls are put into brothels under false names with faked birth certificates. If they are 'insubordinate', the girls are beaten, and they are under constant surveillance. The men hired to keep the girls prisoner are often violent ex-convicts. The girls have access to no sunlight; the windows of the house are darkened, commonly with Venetian blinds that are placed on the exterior of the house, and the rooms sometimes padded to keep anyone from hearing if they scream. If the brothel managers suspect a girl of planning an escape, they sell her to another brothel, sometimes hundreds of miles away.[10]

In this underworld, the clients constantly demand new and increasingly exotic entertainment. At this point, Dyer can't even bear to enumerate, so he summarises the problem thus: 'the nature of which it is impossible to mention in print', though he does mention girls have been imported from central Africa. 'The more childish and innocent the victims, the more profitable they are.'[11]

For whatever reason, Brussels clients had a particular craving for English-speaking girls, which drove a hidden traffic of girls out of England and into the continent. Dyer used his native detective skills to track one such girl who had been trafficked from London to Brussels. Dyer, a Quaker, learned of the girl's plight as he was leaving church. The information trail led to a wealthy Londoner who had recently 'visited' a Brussels brothel. There he met an English girl who told him her story. She had been imprisoned in that establishment, entirely against her will, and she was suicidal. This London informant had left her to her fate, but he did convey the girl's story to Dyer.

The young woman had fallen in love with a man who represented himself as a gentleman and proposed to marry her, if she would accompany him to Belgium. Nineteen and inexperienced, she agreed. Once across the English Channel, her 'fiancé' pretended to run out of money, and he put her under the 'protection' of another man. By this time, the young woman probably had some idea that she was not in a good place. When she resisted the hand-off, her fiancé forced her into a carriage with a trafficker, who took her straight to the brothel. To scrub the kidnapping, she was given a fake name and that name was reported to the government agency that monitored prostitution. Now, she was legally a prostitute in Brussels, kept prisoner in a licensed house fully sanctioned by local authorities, and doing business in the light of day.

Dyer does not disclose to what extent he was the agent in this girl's release. 'Friends' in Belgium were contacted, they found the girl in a hospital, and a Belgian cleric intervened to keep her from being taken straight back to the brothel after her treatment. She returned to London and there Dyer interviewed her himself. Being the good journalist and truth seeker that he was, he fact checked her story with her parents and prior employers. Then he documented his findings in the pages of a London newspaper, withholding the girl's name, of course.[12] This and another trafficking report that Dyer wrote and published flushed several other writers who admitted that they, too, knew of British girls being trafficked to the continent. There were, however, detractors who accused Dyer not only of sensationalism, but of plain making things up. This illustrates the catch-22 that reformers faced in trying to expose child trafficking and kidnapping. It was wickedly easy to throw doubt on an activist's or journalist's testimony because there was so little corroboration. And corroboration was always difficult to find because everyone with a reputation to lose wanted to steer clear of the subject, even in conversation.

The most damaging testimony against Dyer's story came from the Brussels chief of police himself who wrote a letter, published in London, saying every Bruxelloise prostitute had to give testimony at the police station that she was entering the trade of her own free will. Translators were on hand, in case the girl was not a French speaker, the chief declared. No brothel 'keeper' was allowed to be in the room when she gave this declaration. Therefore, no girls could be railroaded into the trade, the chief surmised. London broadsheets also published letters in both English and French insisting that girls could leave the brothels any time they wanted, under the protection of Belgian officials.[13]

A less intrepid do-gooder might have backed down in the face of this spanking and found something easier to do, like basket meals for prisoners and poor families. Dyer doubled down, determined to expose the trafficking ring, and determined to show that the Belgian policy of free agency for prostitutes was routinely suborned.

The most obvious way to expose these kidnappings was also the most dangerous, and not just to Dyer's reputation. Dyer went to Brussels and started visiting brothels, accompanied by two other gentlemen, one Belgian, one English, presumably to ensure unbiased corroboration. He was immediately warned that any attempt to rescue an English girl from a brothel might result in his murder. Ex-convicts guarded the merchandise, and they would not hesitate to employ violence.

During his time in Brussels, Dyer met several English girls being held in brothels under circumstances mostly resembling those of prison. But he focused most of his efforts on a single girl about whom he had heard a report. He entered the brothel where she was residing against her will. As a form of cover, he ordered wine, which he proceeded not to drink. (He was not only a Quaker, but also a teetotaller.) Then he drew out the girl's story.

Her parents had no idea where she was. She came from a decent, rural British family and had held a job at a drapery business in London. There she met a man who represented himself as some kind of doctor. She agreed to have sex with him. Her parents were furious. Her seducer offered to make it up to her by finding her a good job in Brussels, in the same drapery business that she was used to. The drapery shop turned out to be a brothel, and now she was a prisoner there.

Dyer was not one of those journalists who maintains a distance from the story. Flouting the warnings he had received about brothel guards, he did everything he could to free the young lady. And she might have escaped if she had just left the building with him, appearances be damned. But in one of those stranger-than-fiction twists that almost guarantees none of this was made up, her failure to escape came down to clothes. Dyer the Quaker does not tell the reader what she was wearing, as he was interviewing her, but it must have been bad. She refused to walk out onto the street in that attire. She had a box of decent clothes somewhere in the house, but they were under guard. She did not have access to them. To her credit, she also expressed some concern about Dyer's safety. Here, she made her biggest mistake. She asked Dyer to come back the next day when she had figured out her escape.

As far as we know, she never escaped.

What was Dyer to do? Grab a half-dressed, or quarter-dressed, girl and pull her out of the house? He left and talked to his friends. The least dangerous way to extract the prisoner, they all agreed, was to use the judicial system. What followed was a bureaucratic tail chase worthy of Kafka.

Dyer and advocate Alexis Splingard dropped in on the Procureur du Roi, the Belgian equivalent of the crown prosecutor. This official repeated the public line that had been printed in London – the girl was free to leave any time she wanted. Would he at least send a police officer with Dyer to ensure their safety? No. Would he, outside his official capacity, at least write a letter that could put things in motion? No. Dyer and Splingard stated what this procureur surely already knew: that violent men monitored the comings and goings from the brothels. The procureur replied that, if Dyer and Splingard were assaulted, he would 'take cognizance of it'. At that point, Splingard blurted out that, 'in order to be protected in Belgium, we must be killed first'.[14]

Eventually, the procureur referred the men on to the police commissioner, on the promise that the man 'could help us if he pleased'.[15] He did not. The commissioner was not even on the premises when Dyer and Splingard arrived, so they engaged the deputy who was not so cool and collected as the procureur. He repeated that the girl could leave whenever she wanted. Then he had a meltdown which revealed that he knew the exact circumstances under which the girls were held hostage and also defended them: the brothel keepers had made huge capital investments in these places! Then he accused Dyer of being a keeper of a rival brothel, trying to steal the merchandise. Finally, he fled the police station, declaring that he would go see for himself if the girl wanted to leave, but he refused to take Dyer or Splingard with him. Later that day, Dyer was informed that the 'police are so entangled with the keepers of these houses that they cannot be trusted'.[16] Dyer must have felt that this information came a little late as he had already learned it the hard way.

When the deputy returned, declaring that the girl did not want to leave, Dyer had no way of knowing whether he had actually talked to her or not. It seems likely that the deputy did go to the brothel, for the purpose of warning the keeper. Upon returning to the brothel, with his two witnesses, Dyer was greeted by a furious keeper who told him that he could not see the young lady. He was also banned from returning. When Dyer and his witnesses had walked a few steps down the street, a large man chased them down and threatened to break their heads if they returned to the brothel.

At this point, the young English woman was no longer just a newspaper article for Dyer. He worried for her safety, not in the least because a brothel employee had just threatened violence to three gentlemen in the broad light of day in a public place. The temerity and lack of regulation of the brothels was perhaps worse than he had even imagined. What brutality might the unwilling prostitute be subject to, now that it was known she had tried to leave?

Efforts to save this unnamed girl took Dyer to a series of dead ends in the offices of the British Minister, the Vice-Consul, and the Pro-Consul. He returned to England, but kept pursuing the freedom of the girl in Brussels. Brussels officials conducted a sham investigation and published the results in English newspapers, again to prove that English prostitutes were not held prisoner in Belgian brothels.

The Maiden Tribute of Modern Babylon

A few short years later, William Thomas Stead would pick up the gauntlet of exposing sex trafficking, though he concentrated his efforts on the sex trade in London. Stead was a complicated man who is said, by some, to be the inventor of tabloid journalism. That is rarely meant as a compliment, and it may serve as an attempt to minimise his accomplishments. Stead's writing was frequently much more florid than it needed to be, and he often seemed to joyously revel in his terrible subject matter, much like a child who finds an apple covered in maggots. So it behoves any examination of Stead's investigations to report, up front, that he was highly instrumental in raising the British legal age of consent, under which an individual can have sex, from 13 to 16. That legal reform was actually called the Stead Act. And while a mere act of law could not stop Victorian men from raping children – kidnapping and assault were already illegal and the laws of the age should have stopped it – at least it sent a message that children should not be having sex. As a newspaper editor, he advocated for other things that would, eventually, prevent the Oliver Twists and Nancies of the world from their worst fates. These were compulsory primary and secondary education and equal treatment for women.

Stead exposed the worst aspects of the London sex trade in a series of articles in the *Pall Mall Gazette*. The series ran under the unfortunate title *The Maiden Tribute of Modern Babylon*. That title alludes to a myth that says, after losing a war, the city of Athens, Greece was obliged to send fourteen children to Crete every nine years. In this obvious precursor to the *Hunger Games*, when the children arrived by boat in Crete, they were cast into the labyrinth of the minotaur. There, they wandered until the minotaur found and killed them. Stead really liked this analogy and spent quite a bit of time developing it. The children that got caught up in the London sex trade were like the children who get sacrificed to the minotaur. 'Maidens they were when this morning dawned, but to-night their ruin will be accomplished, and tomorrow they will find themselves within the portal of the maze of London brotheldom,' he wrote to clarify the comparison.[17] Stead may have felt that bringing a fine Hellenic analogy to his writing would give it some cachet. If people don't talk about the *Maiden Tribute* as much as they ought to, it's probably because of the title and its cumbersome analogy.

Stead did much of his research for the *Maiden Tribute* undercover, and his undercover work was his great accomplishment as a journalist. The Victorians did not even yet have a word for undercover journalism, so Stead referred to his series and the people who worked with him to uncover information as a 'secret commission'. He began his research well-armed with a knowledge of the law as it pertained to the sex trade in England. Without an understanding of how little Victorian law protected children, it is impossible to comprehend the child sex trade in that era.

First, the age of consent was 13. As Stead noted, girls of that age sometimes didn't even know the mechanics of sex. Very often, they had deliberately been kept in ignorance by parents who thought knowledge would lead to experience. A 13- or 14-year-old could be offered a sovereign to 'go into that room and do as the gentleman asks'. Afterwards, it was impossible to prove rape. She had gone into the room willingly and agreed, in advance, to whatever happened.

Second, the law did not acknowledge a rape had happened if the girl was lied to or lured into a building against her interests. If a 14-year-old consented to have sex with a man who promised to marry her or to provide her with a respectable job, and then he dumped her at a brothel, she had no case in court. Stead often refers to the *Digest of the Criminal Law*, a sort of law for dummies, written by James Fitzjames Stephen. When Stephen had digested the sprawling laws of England, it turned out that, 'where consent is obtained by fraud the act does not amount to rape although the woman may not have been aware of the nature of the act.'[18]

Finally, brothels were all about protecting the reputations of their clients. If a man had to rape a girl to have sex with her, the brothel keeper and other staff members would all swear the sex had been consensual. The act had happened in a private room with no witnesses. Therefore, it was her word against his, and brothel keepers were quick to tell their victims that no one would 'have them', i.e. marry or employ them, now that they had been 'ruined'. Keepers even assured raped girls that their parents would not want them now.

Stead started his investigation by interviewing a policeman who assured him that the sex trade in girls was flourishing and that virgins could be 'obtained' for sex very easily. When Stead asked if the girls understood what they were doing, the policeman seemed surprised. 'Of course they are rarely willing, and as a rule they do not know what they are coming for.'[19] Stead next asked the very uncomfortable question, 'But do the girls cry out?'[20] Of course they did, the policeman said. But the police have no right to intervene, he explained. If a policeman barged into a house every time a woman screamed, he would frequently be interfering with a pregnant woman's delivery of a child.

Like a good journalist, Stead had follow-up questions. Could the girl or her parents not prosecute? Well, no, because all was arranged so that she never knew the name of her assailant. Furthermore, a girl, however young, who has lost her 'virtue' would be a discredited witness. Just the fact that she had been in a brothel 'would possibly be held to be evidence of her consent'.[21]

Next, Stead interviewed a man that he described as an 'expert' and 'specialist', read 'brothel client'. This man denied that virgin children were taken to brothels. Instead, he insisted, their parents sold them directly to men who had a 'taste' for them.[22]

Stead's next confidential interview was with a man who had worked at a brothel, but had repudiated the business and was now attempting to live a more honest life. This man had gone out in the 'field', so to speak, and recruited prostitutes fraudulently. He admitted to travelling long distances to bring in a 'mark'. His method of operation was to court these girls and get engaged to them. He used a number of disguises, sometimes dressing as a parson. On a promise of marriage, the girls would travel with him to London. There, he would ply them with food and drink, heavy on the drink. Then they would 'miss' their last train, and he would take them to the brothel without disclosing the business nature of it. When a girl was alone in her room, he sent in the 'gentleman' with whom he had an arrangement. Afterwards, the girl usually consented to be a sex worker.

This source also said that the daughters of prostitutes are often raised to serve the purpose of selling their virginity. At 12 or 13, they were merchantable. The former brothel worker recounted that he had once procured a 12-year-old virgin for a clergyman who had come to his house to hand out religious tracts. The clergyman paid £20.[23]

Stead interviewed another reformed brothel keeper who had got into the work by way of prostitution. The woman told the story of how she had tracked a 13-year-old and hired her as a maid. Then she whisked the girl off to London, away from the mother who had agreed that she should be a domestic servant. She sold the girl's virginity for £13, and her client had sex with the child while she was in a drugged sleep. The former brothel keeper discussed several methods of drugging a virgin. Some people used chloroform, she explained, but her drugs of choice were laudanum and snuff. The girl would wake up in pain the next morning, and the brothel keeper would have a very matter-of-fact conversation with her. Yes, she had lost her virginity, as everyone must. She had lost her character, and now no one would take her in. She was welcome to stay as a house attraction. If she did not consent, the brothel keeper threatened to throw her out on the streets with nothing. Most of the time, 'the child who is usually under fifteen, frightened and friendless, her head aching with the effect of the drowse and full of pain and horror, gives up all hope' and accepts her new profession.[24] It was the law of supply and demand, the former brothel keeper explained. 'If they want a maid we must get them one, or they will go elsewhere. We cannot afford to lose their custom.'[25]

An informant in East London then told Stead of a house, not of prostitution, but where a midwife prepared certificates of virginity. According to Stead's research, certificates of virginity were issued by doctors and midwives. It absolutely *must* be noted that twentieth-century science has rendered these certificates bogus. Setting the horrific uses made of these documents carefully over to one side, doctors and scientists tell us that there is no way to perfectly detect whether a girl or boy has ever had sex. Disgusted by honour killings and artificial replacement hymens, the usually austere National Institutes of Health have issued a report titled, 'Is my daughter still a virgin? Can you, please, check it, doctor?' that says, no, no, we can't. 'There is no physical sign that indicates the virginity of a woman … the hymen is an anatomical part, an elastic membrane in the vaginal canal … It is sufficiently elastic to be penetrated without breaking, but fragile [enough] to be lacerated by activities other than sexual interactions.'[26]

Stead apparently believed in the validity of virgin certification. He may, therefore, have exaggerated the number of innocents who were raped by men voracious for virgins. Stead was aware that experienced girls could be passed off as virgins to satisfy defloration mania. He referred to this several times as 'vamping a girl up' to imitate a virgin. Of course, the procurers and brothel keepers he interviewed denied ever doing such a thing and pointed to the certificates as proof. There is small comfort to take from knowing that not all raped virgins were virgins. This does nothing to mitigate the fact that violence against children was occurring, or that the same child was subjected to similar violence over and over again.

Belief in the hymen was strong in the nineteenth century. Many doctors and midwives handed out certificates of virginity when all they could really tell was whether or not a girl had recently had sex rough enough to leave an injury. Why did they certify virginity when it is impossible to do so? The obvious answer is to give the customer what he wants. Doing so was more likely to bring in repeat business. In his research, Stead would eventually stumble upon evidence that virginity certificates were not reliable. But he seems not to have heeded it.

The midwife Stead interviewed ran a sort of one-stop shop for prostitutes. She not only performed the bogus virginity tests, but also treated girls with injuries received from their rapists. She performed abortions, as well. Stead did not visit this establishment himself, but he recorded the testimony of his 'agent' who went there and interviewed the midwife. This woman did not entertain brothel clients in her home, but she did know where someone could find a child to have sex with. With horrific coolness, she told of a man she knew who stalked girls. He waited for them to come out of the shops and factories, where they worked, at lunchtime. He would see a girl that took his fancy and make her acquaintance. Then, when she trusted him, he would propose a little trip. When he had her at a distance from her support circle, he

Though Fagin, pictured here on the left, is a fictional character, many criminal child gangs did have invisible adults guiding them. (*Public domain*)

This beautifully executed drawing of the Saint Marylebone Workhouse was drawn by one of its inmates in 1866. (*Creative Commons*)

This extremely accurate watercolor, by J. P. Emslie, depicts the inside of Saint Marylebone workhouse. It was created in 1898. (*Creative Commons*)

This etching by George Cruikshank captures the pivotal moment when Oliver Twist braves the workhouse beadle to ask for more porridge. (*Wellcome Collection*)

Pictured here is the Foundling Hospital where babies and even small children could be dropped off anonymously by their guardians. They were left on the outdoor steps of the building, often in baskets. (*Wikimedia Commons*)

London's Newgate Prison loomed as a warning to anyone engaged in even the pettiest of crimes. It was famous for its inhumane conditions. George Shepherd drew the original of this print around 1810. (*Wikimedia Commons*)

Jackie Coogan starred as Oliver Twist in a 1922 adaptation of Charles Dickens's novel. Coogan's costume aptly captures the ways boys dressed in the Victorian age. The notion that children should wear clothing different from adults had not yet emerged. The real Oliver Twists simply wore smaller versions of what adult men wore, right down to the top hats. (*Wikimedia Commons*)

This political cartoon, drawn by W. A. Rogers in 1903, lampoons affluent industry barons whose wealth was built by poorly paid and undernourished children. (*Wikimedia Commons*)

The artist of this engraving is unknown. On the left, a sweep, darkened by the soot of his trade, is presumably engaging his customers. (*Wikimedia Commons*)

Picking apart old ropes to make oakum was a brutal occupation that burned and cut the hands of people who did it. This was the work that Oliver Twist and his fellow children were set to. Such work was also assigned to prisoners like those pictured here in the Middlesex House of Correction. (*Wikimedia Commons*)

This illustration by William Hogarth shows a young woman being recruited into prostitution by a cynical madam. Hanging from the younger woman's right arm are thread and other sewing implements. She had come to London hoping to find work as a seamstress. (*Wikimedia Commons*)

This illustration by Joseph Clayton Clark depicts Dickens's 'Artful Dodger' character. The dodger is simultaneously a child and an experienced criminal. As such, he represents the gangs of child criminals that occupied London for centuries, having been driven to crime by abandonment and homelessness. (*Wikimedia Commons*)

Though *Oliver Twist* forefronts its innocent male protagonist, the character of Nancy is also a poignant depiction of a child who falls into a life of crime through the agency of a cynical and exploitative adult. Here, actress Otten Olssen portrays Nancy. (*Wikimedia Commons*)

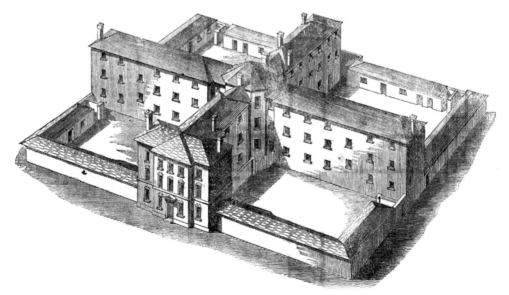

The poor law commission, which made recommendations leading to the Poor Law Amendment Act, illustrated their findings with this design for a poor house. Men and women were to be separately housed in different wings. (*Public domain*)

This scathing illustration, by the caricaturist Phiz, shows hungry children as well as adults, both abled and disabled, receiving grudging charity from a workhouse. (Courtesy of Wellcome Library via *Creative Commons*)

Philosopher Jeremy Bentham directly influenced the poor laws of the Victorian era. His belief that people were essentially lazy and would prefer to live on charity rather than working underpinned the needless harshness of workhouses. He wrote, in effect, that individual welfare could be sacrificed, as needed, to 'the greatest happiness of the greatest number'. (*Public domain*)

Thomas Robert Malthus, pictured here, theorised that the world's population would outgrow its resources unless checked. In his opinion, this justified making life hard for the poor. The poor needed to be incentivised to work hard, stay independent, and limit family size. Malthus's work underpinned the Poor Law Amendment Act of 1834. (*Public domain*)

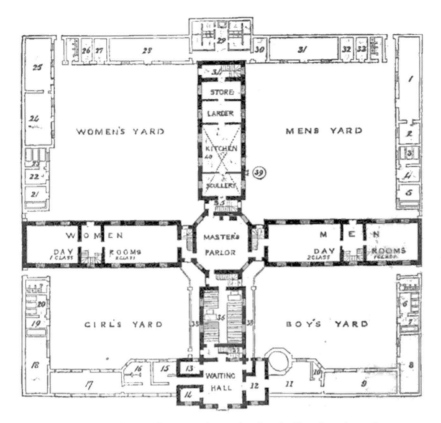

The floor plan of a model workhouse illustrates the cruelty that the Poor Law Amendment was prepared to enact. The amendment made it possible to break up families, separating husbands and wives and brothers and sisters into segregated wings. (*Public domain*)

Here a child or young adult is pictured hauling a coal tub up a mine shaft. (*Public domain*)

Charles Dickens, author of *Oliver Twist*, was himself a victim of childhood poverty and exploitation. When his father was sent to debtor's prison, Dickens was sent to work at a boot blacking factory. He was 12 years old when he began this work, and he missed three years of school while working full time under harsh conditions. (*Public domain*)

The children pictured here are working with fibres at a London hosiery mill in Tennessee. In his day, photographer Lewis Hine was reviled as a muckraker for exposing child labour with photographs like these. But his work led to laws limiting child labour in the United States. (*Wikimedia*)

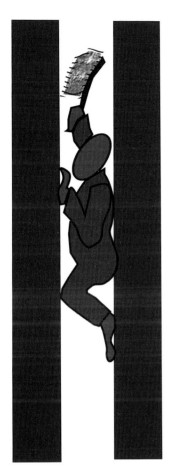

As this illustration shows, sweeps could easily become stuck in chimneys if they were not careful how they climbed. The boy to the right is wedged into a 9 inch by 14 inch chimney. Such children had to be somehow pulled out or the chimney would have to be broken to retrieve their dead bodies. (*Illustration courtesy of Clem Rutter, Rochester, Kent. Wikimedia*)

Pictured here is a makeshift hospital ward located in a Liverpool workhouse. (*Wellcome*)

Victorian novelist Frances Trollope wrote about the travails of the poor in Great Britain. This illustration depicts a disabled elderly character, named old Sally, in Trollope's novel *Michael Armstrong*. The main character is a factory boy who is lifted out of poverty by a twist of good fortune. (*Public domain*)

This poignant image, by the artist Herviue, accompanied the story of Michael Armstrong in Frances Trollope's novel about a 9-year-old boy who worked in a factory to support his sick mother and disabled brother. (*Public domain*)

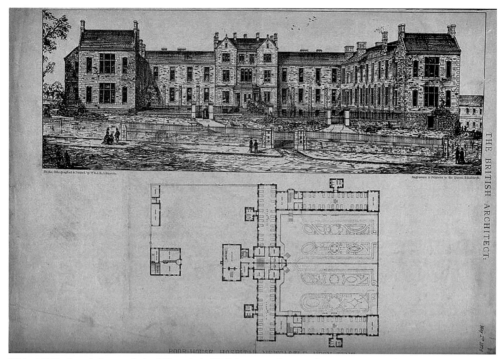

This 1874 photolithograph, by W. and A. K. Johnston, depicts the exterior and floor plan of the poor house hospital in Newcastle-Upon-Tyne. (*Public domain*)

MR. CHARLES DICKENS'S LAST READING.

Prolific novelist Charles Dickens drew on his own troubled childhood in writing *Oliver Twist*. He is pictured here reading from his fiction. (*Public domain*)

THE POOR PICKING THE BONES TO LIVE

The Poor Law Amendment manifested its logical conclusion at the Andover Workhouse where the poor were put on starvation wages and set to work crushing bones into fertiliser. The starving workers understandably resorted to sucking the marrow from the bones they were crushing and even fighting over bones. This 1845 illustration from the *Penny Satirist* brought the deprivation of Andover residents to light. (*Public domain*)

William Thomas Stead was a journalist and advocate for children's welfare. His *Maiden Tribute of Modern Babylon* exposed the underbelly of child trafficking and child prostitution and led to reforms that bore his name. (*Public domain*)

Victorian reformer Annie Besant was critical to the success of the Bryant & May matchstick workers' strike. (*Creative Commons*)

A MERRY CHRISTMAS AND A HAPPY NEW YEAR.

John Leighton's lithograph of a chimney sweep waiting at a doctor's door. (*Public domain*)

The children in this illustration are factory workers, pictured here supplementing their bleak diets with pig fodder, as did Robert Blincoe. (*Creative Commons*)

Children picking cotton in a cotton factory. (*Creative Commons*)

A ragged school in Whitechapel. (*Public domain*)

In this photograph of Bryant & May matchstick girls, at least two of the workers pictured show signs of phossy jaw. Workers absorbed white phosphorus from the factory, and it caused slow but steady deterioration of the jaw bone. (*Public domain*)

raped her, and the midwife had another patient to treat for lacerations. 'I do not know how many I have had to repair after him,' she said.[27]

Stead revisited the question why the cries of assaulted children do not draw more scrutiny after one or two of his under-reporters interviewed the keeper of a fashionable 'villa'. The keeper seems to have actually shown Stead's agent the room where virgins would be raped. The keeper pointed out that the house was free standing, the walls thick, the floor double carpeted, and the single window had heavy curtains on the inside and shutters on the outside. Stead's agent then asked the uncomfortable but necessary question, 'What if the child is actually killed in the process?' The keeper then vehemently denied that that was possible. 'You will not kill her … you have too much sense to kill the girl. Anything short of that, you can do as you please.'[28] Stead also found evidence that, in a suburban London brothel, the keeper had taken the precaution of employing straps when she had a girl that might resist: 'whenever the girl was fourteen or fifteen years of age she should be strapped down hand and foot to the four posts of the bedstead.'[29]

According to Stead's report, brothels were constantly on the aggressive lookout for new prostitutes. A small, less affluent brothel keeper would do the recruitment herself, but the wealthier ones had staff members dedicated to that work. These recruiters would stalk vulnerable young women everywhere they could find them. They trawled the workhouses, they met first-time prisoners right outside the prison doors on the moment of their release. They researched servant registries. They even infiltrated 'Magdalen houses'. 'They have been known to profess penitence in order to gain access to a home for fallen women, where they thought some Magdalens repenting of their penitence might be secured for their house.'[30]

In the course of his research, Stead often went through the first steps of procuring a woman for sex. That is to say he contacted someone who was in the sex trade, asked for a 'maid', and, in many cases, even got around to meeting the girl. His pursuit ended there or at the doctor's office. Most readers will find it distasteful that Stead engaged himself so deeply in that underworld. So we must remember that this was a culture that was denied by the mainstream. Anything less than deep cover would not have exposed the practices so thoroughly.

In order to conduct a prolonged interview with two women he identified as Mesdames X and Z, Stead posed as a man wishing to purchase the services of several virgins. Mesdames X and Z were, he had learned, full-time procurers. They did not run a house. They were middlemen in the truest sense of the word. Both had other jobs and one still lived with her parents, providing cover for their illicit activities. Over the course of several days, X and Z presented Stead with girls. The first child that X and Z brought Stead was a 14-year-old whose mother had just died. She came from a rural area and had been sent to Oxford Street to learn dressmaking. Under the terms of a typical apprenticeship, she made no money. She could read very little and could not write at all. In arranging introductions, X and Z routinely told the girls that all they had to do to earn a high sum was 'play a game' with a gentleman. They also told girls that they could not get pregnant on the first sexual encounter. Upon meeting this teen, Stead observed that the girl 'had only the vaguest idea of what was involved in meeting a gentleman'. Nevertheless, X and Z had brought her to him with the promise that she agreed to be seduced. This girl went to the midwife to be 'tested' for virginity. At one point, she believed she had fulfilled her seduction contract with the test, because the test itself was somewhat painful.[31]

X and Z admitted in so many words that they did not allow a contracted girl to change her mind. They related the chilling story of a girl who wrapped herself up in some curtains to protect herself. They ended up holding her down for their client. But to prevent last-minute cancellations, they preferred to threaten the girl. If she fought, she would be seduced anyway, but not paid, they explained.

Procuring was a long game, X and Z admitted. They were typically up and dressed by seven in the morning, when they started the day trolling for marks in Hyde and Green Parks. In the afternoons, they looked for girls in Regent's Park. They looked for nurses, i.e. young girls put in charge of strolling babies. Cooks and governesses also made good providers. 'It takes time, patience, and experience,' they bragged. 'Many girls need months before they can be brought in. You need to proceed very cautiously at first.'[32]

Stead next asked for a package deal of five virgins, to be 'retailed' to his friends. But this time, he insisted that the girls first go to a doctor of his choosing. This unnamed man was a real doctor, but he was also undercover with Stead, a sympathiser who wished to expose the child sex trade. Over the course of a report that is often hard to read, it transpires, finally, that Stead's goal here was to get everything in writing. Of course, he never intended to have sex with these girls, but in playing out the charade, he learned a great deal about how the sex trade worked. He made a point of paying the girls the money they had been promised. Then, importantly, he came away with documents certifying virginity and with contracts in which the girls agreed to meet him at any address he specified and have sex with him. The language of the contract was 'let you have me'.[33] Stead understood that, without documentation, he could be accused of overdramatising and even fabrication.

X and Z complied with his request by bringing three girls to Stead's doctor. One was 16, the other two were younger and worked in shops. Stead's doctor certified only the 16-year-old. Because he worked for Stead, this man had no reason to pretend that virginity can really be detected. About the other two girls, he said it could go either way. The procurers were determined to meet the quota, though, so they kept turning up with more girls, three of whom were 14. Stead wished to interview at least some of these girls, but he found that they had given false addresses, under the instruction of X and Z, who did that to safeguard their commission.

Finally, though, Stead was able to interview two of these girls. The first one seemed, at least to the reader, to have some idea what she was in for. Her father was dead, her mother was an alcoholic. She needed the money. The procurers had told her she couldn't get pregnant, though she seemed to understand that was a lie. She had decided to give the baby up or drown herself in the event of a pregnancy. After this interview, Stead sent her into a room where a female friend of his would attend to her. He then interviewed the second girl.

She was 16. Her mother was a charwoman, her father was mentally ill. She earned 5 shillings a week working in a millinery. They were very poor, and she needed the £2 she had been promised. She was in tears for much of the interview. It emerged that the thing she feared most was being undressed. She had most certainly not been briefed on the physiological process of being seduced. She would 'lose her maid', she had been told. She did not fear pregnancy because 'having a baby doesn't come of being seduced, does it?'[34]

Stead persisted in providing the girl with a more scientific sex education than she had had from parents or procurers. Seduction would be painful. To have sex under these circumstances was shameful. (Stead never could transcend the double standard pertaining to sexual experience. We can possibly forgive him for this on the grounds that having sex for money does not usually boost self-esteem.) Yes, she could get pregnant from a seduction, even a first one, Stead explained. In the course of this conversation, it emerged that Z had been grooming the girl by giving her a shilling here and there and also giving money to her mother. The tearful girl estimated that Z had given her family about 30 shillings altogether. She believed herself in debt. And her family was 'so poor'.[35]

Stead pointed out that the cost of raising a child would be much more of a financial hardship than foregoing £2 now would be. Perhaps without realising it, the writer had stumbled upon the reality that the desperately poor rarely have any ability to prioritise the future over the present. He did, however, understand that such a 16-year-old was not liable for any mistake she might make in this arena: 'Could any proof be more conclusive as to the absolute inability of this girl of sixteen to form an estimate of the value of the only commodity with which the law considers her amply able to deal the day after she is thirteen?'[36]

Dickens and Urania Cottage

For the careful reader, Nancy may evoke the most compassion out of all the characters in *Oliver Twist*. The Artful Dodger is deported, leaving the reader to hope he will find a new and more legitimate outlet for his ingenuity. Oliver is saved – by his innate virtue, but also by an accident of birth. But Nancy comes to a violent and early end, as so many of the Nancies did. And her violent end is undeserved, even by Victorian standards which so often blamed the victim. She dies saving Oliver from Fagin's gang, not as an outcome of 'vice'.

Dickens understood that girls like Nancy were the worst victims of an age that threw away its young people, when they could not present good parents. We know that the author had a particular sense of mission to such girls because he established a sanctuary, called Urania Cottage, for the Nancies. Funding for the cottage came from Baroness Angela Georgina Burdett-Coutts. The purpose of the cottage was to offer safety and education to young women from workhouses, prisons, and the street. Today, we would call Urania Cottage a 'transitional' accommodation. The idea was to, first, separate young 'fallen' women from the toxic environments that could be difficult to leave because of habit and lack of options, second, to treat them with kindness, and finally give them skills useful for another way of life.

In 1849, Dickens wrote his pamphlet titled 'Appeal to Fallen Women'. The purpose of this pamphlet was to invite the Fallen Women to Urania Cottage. It is clear that Dickens hoped to get the pamphlet directly into the hands of young women on the streets and in prison. We know little about the pamphlet's direct results, who received it, and whether it actually made it into the prisons, but that was the intention.

The pamphlet has, perhaps justly, been criticised for a tone of condescension and an unconscious sense of entitlement. To be fair, Dickens did incorporate some meta-commentary that aimed to defuse the tone of condescension: 'And do not think that I write to you as if I felt myself very much above you, or wished to hurt your feelings by reminding you of the situation in which you are placed. God forbid!

I mean nothing but kindness to you, and I write as if you were my sister.'[37] The attempt to seem less superior fails, of course, but at least it was made.

However, the power of Dickens's writing, his ability to immediately engage the emotions of his reader, is evident in the words: 'I address it to a woman – a very young woman still – who was born to be happy and has lived miserably; who has no prospect before her but sorrow, or behind her but a wasted youth; who, if she has ever been a mother, has felt shame instead of pride in her own unhappy child.'[38]

The essay lays out, in fairly specific terms, the difficulties of growing old in the oldest profession. It does not shy away from the risks of disease, mental illness, and suicide.

It becomes clear, as the essay progresses, that Dickens thinks the best destiny of the street walker is to learn to be a housewife and then, leave Britain: 'they will be supplied with every means, when some time shall have elapsed and their conduct shall have fully proved their earnestness and reformation, to go abroad, where in a distant country they may become the faithful wives of honest men, and live and die in peace.'[39] Apparently, neither Dickens nor Burdett-Coutts thought a girl could leave her reputation behind anywhere in Britain. It is an indication of how much judgement a Victorian street girl, not technically even breaking the law, could receive that she had to go to an entirely different continent in order to shake off her past.

Chapter 5

From the Brothel to the Baby Farm: Child Abduction

Victorian trafficking in children was mostly unregulated, and children born to poor families had almost no protection under the law. There were at least three ways a child of 13 or even younger could be parted from his or her family: abduction, sale, and baby farming.

Abduction

William Thomas Stead cited numerous cases of children being abducted in his article series *The Maiden Tribute of Modern Babylon*. The most compelling example he gives is of a child brothel operating under the name 'The Infant School'. The child sex workers employed at this establishment were aged 12 to 15. Stead gives no details of their abduction, most likely because there were no records of such. But that the children were abducted was obvious because multiple mothers of those children were trying to get their kids back. Not only would the brothel not release the children to their mothers, the mothers did not even get to see their offspring.[1]

The only law applicable to child abduction was 'habeas corpus'. This law stipulated two things that made child abduction particularly lucrative. First, it imposed an inscrutable twenty-four-hour waiting period before a premises could be entered for the purpose of liberating a child. So, even if a parent could afford the financial burden of recovering her child through the law, the abductor could easily move the child to another location within the twenty-four-hour window. The law, in fact, seems to have been written for the specific benefit of child traffickers.

The second and most prohibitive consideration was the cost of proving child abduction. Stead estimated that it cost parents a minimum of £30 to bring a charge of habeas corpus. When the annual salary of a common labourer, working ten-hour days, six days a week, was approximately £10 a year or less, recovering an abducted child was about as likely as a free trip on Elon Musk's space ship.

Today, multiple law enforcement agencies swing into action if a child does not come home from school. And it should have been the case that Victorian police would vigilantly pursue and prosecute child abductions. But, according to Stead, police were more likely to collude in such crimes. Brothel keepers and sex workers themselves routinely 'tipped' the police. In fact, if such bribes were not forthcoming, a sex worker would be driven out of London, Stead avers: 'if a girl were once to tip and tell she might just as well leave London at once. She would be harried out of division after division, and never allowed to rest until she was outside the radius of the metropolitan district.'[2]

The collaboration between brothels and the police was more formalised. 'Every brothel becomes more or less a source of revenue to the policemen on the beat,' Stead wrote. One brothel keeper confessed to paying the police £3 a week, but immediately noted that his was a small business. The larger brothels, this source stated, paid upwards of £500 a year.[3]

The police were such formidable foes of justice that, when word got abroad that the *Pall Mall Gazette* was publishing articles about sex trafficking, the police allowed rioters to descend on the newspaper's offices. Windows were broken, the premises were violently trespassed. Stead notes that Lord Aberdeen, then prime minister of the United Kingdom, had a clear view of the damages from his office across the street. Printing was delayed by three hours while staff were unable to enter or leave the newspaper offices.[4]

The story of the 'Infant School' has a happy ending, however. The children were saved, but not because anyone could be convicted of abduction. Luckily, the proprietor was so brazen, he did not bother keeping up the paperwork on liquor sales. On this point, the short arm of the law swung into action, raided the establishment, and reunited the stolen children with their parents.[5]

Sale

The sale of Eliza Armstrong proved that selling a child in England was permissible, but, under some circumstances, buying a child was not. To prove how easily a child could be sold into prostitution, William Thomas Stead orchestrated the purchase of Eliza, a 13-year-old, through undercover agents. In his articles, he used a fake name, 'Lily', to protect Eliza's identity.

Stead recruited Rebecca Jarrett, a reformed prostitute and procurer, into his investigative team. Jarrett's story is of interest to scholars of Victorian poverty and deserves more research independently of her connection to Stead's investigation. She was the youngest of seven children who were abandoned by their father. Her alcoholic mother put Rebecca to work as a prostitute at the age of 12. At that time, British law allowed 12-year-olds to be sex workers. Eventually, Jarrett herself became a procurer, recruiting children as sex workers. However, Jarrett developed a conscience about this work and threw herself on the mercy of Florence Booth, a lieutenant in the Salvation Army. Booth took her in, giving her an out from prostitution and procuring. Jarrett had been 'reformed' for less than a year when she went undercover for Stead.

She may or may not have known just how dangerous it would be to go into her old world as Stead's investigator. She had absolutely no protection, should things go wrong, and they did. She would pay a very high price – six months in prison doing hard labour – for helping Stead bring the truth of child trafficking into the light of day. As such, Jarrett should probably be considered the hero of the Eliza Armstrong case.

Under Stead's direction, Jarrett used her old contacts in the criminal world. She inquired about the purchase of a young teenager for the purpose of setting up a new brothel, of which the purchased child would be the star. While negotiations were afoot, Elizabeth Armstrong got wind of them and offered to sell her 13-year-old daughter, named Eliza, to Jarrett. Stead wrote that Elizabeth Armstrong knew her daughter would be turned into a sex worker, and she was anxious to conduct the sale. Eliza's father, a chimney sweeper, was informed of the impending sale, and he offered no objection. Both parents were alcoholics, according to the *Maiden Tribute*. Elizabeth handed Eliza over to Stead's agent for a sovereign. The agent then sold the girl on to a procurer for £5, two of which were withheld until the girl's virginity was 'certified'. Louise Mourez, a midwife and abortionist, certified Eliza's virginity, noting that she was very small and would experience a great deal of pain. She sold a vial of chloroform to make the assault on Eliza more tolerable.[6]

Stead's account of all this in the *Pall Mall Gazette* is deeply flawed. He offers details of the girl's appearance – 'slightly coarse in texture, with dark black eyes, and short, sturdy figure' – and quotes a poem that she wrote, not realising, apparently, that such details might appear salacious to some readers.[7]

Even more troublingly, Stead gave in to the temptation that all journalists face at one point or another: he made something up because the story wasn't sensational enough. Historians all agree that Stead rescued Eliza before any assault could occur, and Eliza's sworn testimony before a court of law indicates that she was never raped. But Stead wrote her story as if she *had* been sexually assaulted:

The door opened, and the purchaser entered the bedroom. He closed and locked the door. There was a brief silence. And then there rose a wild and piteous cry, not a loud shriek, but a helpless, startled scream like the bleat of a frightened lamb. And the child's voice was heard crying, in accents of terror, 'There's a man in the room. Take me home; oh, take me home!'
And then all once more was still.[8]

The actual facts of the Eliza Armstrong abduction are these: the child was taken to a brothel, where she undressed and got into bed. Stead entered the room, and Eliza screamed that there was a man in the room. Stead then left the room, content that he had proven that Eliza could have been raped.

An important tactical error that Stead and Jarrett made was to deploy the chloroform that Mourez had sold them. According to Stead, he attempted to use the chloroform because he did not want Eliza to be frightened. However, having got a whiff of the substance on a handkerchief, Eliza refused to put it to her face, and no one forced it on her. Eliza's testimony supported this account. But the attempt to drug a child featured heavily in the summons that dragged Jarrett and Stead through the court system and the media.

Stead's very yellow reportage did not help his case when the crown charged him and his fellow investigators with procuring and abduction. By that time, rival newspapers had investigated Stead's story. They discovered that 'Lily' was a fake name, and that Stead had played a much larger role in the story than he had revealed in his article. It could be construed from the facts that Stead was both the purchaser and the theoretical rapist.

When police interviewed Armstrong's parents, they absolutely denied Stead's version of events and offered their own contradictory version. Her father claimed that he was not consulted about the sale. This turned out to be an important point of law. A daughter was her father's property and could not be taken without his permission. Elizabeth admitted to turning Eliza over to Jarrett, but claimed that Jarrett promised to put the girl into domestic service, not into prostitution. Stead was not an actual witness to the sale, so he could offer no eyewitness testimony that the parents had conspired to sell their daughter into prostitution.

For exposing vice, Stead and Jarrett stood accused of committing vice. The irony here was not lost on Stead, and he did not waste any time getting this injustice into print: 'I am charged with conspiracy. What I did was to expose a conspiracy ... we stand here accused of ... crimes with which even our worst enemies do not pretend that we have the slightest sympathy,' he wrote. 'It is because the knowledge that they were being committed with impunity all around us, burned like fire in our brain, and would not let us rest night or day, that we were driven to those methods which have landed us in the position we occupy at this hour.'[9]

Stead also made the salient point that the police showed no interest in the actual content of the *Maiden Tribute* after it was published. They never contacted him for more information, nor did they even pretend to launch their own investigation. The police only became interested in Stead when he, himself, fell under suspicion as a procurer.

Rebecca Jarrett, on whose testimony Stead had based his article, was an activist with the Salvation Army at the time she became an undercover investigator for Stead. In his court testimony, Stead defended Jarrett with all the ammunition that words alone can supply. He had been reluctant to employ her, but he could not have exposed child trafficking without her help. 'I was … reluctantly obliged to employ Rebecca Jarrett in a transaction for which I alone ought to have borne the full legal, as I certainly bear the full moral, responsibility.'[10] Stead also clarified that Jarrett had been reluctant to involve herself in his investigations, but that she had been moved by the moral imperative of the mission.

However, the court ruled that the motivation of the defendants was irrelevant. This left Jarrett without the moral attribute of working undercover to expose vice. She was tried and sentenced as a known child procurer who had abducted and procured yet another child. Jarrett survived her six months of hard labour and went back to working with the Salvation Army upon her release.

Stead was sentenced to only three months, and, by severe contrast with Jarrett, he was treated as a celebrity prisoner. He had his own room, his family were allowed to spend Christmas Day with him there, he mostly wore his own civilian clothing, and he even had a servant who was hired from among the other convicts. As any good journalist would, he used the experience as fodder for his writing. Having been imprisoned in the course of unveiling the hideous truth about child trafficking gave him even more bragging rights than before.

There is little doubt that Jarrett's and Stead's intervention in Eliza Armstrong's life transformed it for the better. After the famous scream, she was whisked off to safety by the Salvation Army. They found her a place in the Princess Louise Home for the Protection of Young Girls in Wanstead, Essex. There she trained as a domestic servant and eventually took a job as a nursemaid to the children of architect Charles Clement Hodges in Hexham Northumberland. Records from 1893 find her married to Henry George West, a gas fitter and plumber. They lived in South Shields and had at least three children prior to his death in 1906.

Eliza was a widow for no more than five years. By 1911, she had married Samuel O'Donnell, a lead worker from Donegal. They lived in Jarrow where Eliza had four more children while still raising the children from her marriage with West. She outlived O'Donnell and died, at 66, in 1938. Eliza would never again be an entirely private person. Her story hit a public nerve, and newspapers found readers keen to learn her fate. Fascination with Eliza continued well into the twenty-first century when the British Library published a series of articles about her and asked for further information.

Still, Eliza Armstrong's loss of privacy may have been a small price to pay for the destiny that she escaped. We cannot know exactly what would have become of her, had Stead not intervened in her fate. But we do know these facts: following Eliza's removal from her home, both her parents were arrested, her father for beating up a neighbour, her mother for hitting a woman with a broom and kicking a policeman. Elizabeth served fourteen days in prison. As chronic alcoholics do, Charles Armstrong started hearing voices and was eventually declared insane. He ended his days in the Colney Hatch Asylum in 1890. Eliza's brother, John, was arrested for begging at the age of 12 and ended up in a workhouse. Far from standing as a character witness, his mother testified that he was a 'bad boy'. She admitted to beating him, starving him, and withholding his clothing, all in an effort to make him behave, but none of these sterling parenting techniques had proven effective, she declared in court.[11]

Eliza has many points in common with Oliver Twist. She is the victim of a system that enslaves children to the hardest and most unpleasant work there is. The adults responsible for her care see her as an asset to be sold to the highest bidder rather than a child to be raised with love and care. But the most obvious similarity is the deus ex machina ending that saves both children. Oliver turns out to be the legitimate member of a wealthy family. He is more raptured than rescued out of the streets and a life of crime. If she had not had the great good luck to be William Thomas Stead's cautionary tale, Eliza might well have become a prostitute for real. To dull the psychological pain of such a life, she might well have followed in her parents' alcoholic footsteps. She might have followed them into prison. She might have died at a young age, diseased, exhausted. If she were a fictional character in a novel, we might say that her happy ending was far too contrived.

But she is not a fictional character. She was a very lucky woman, the beneficiary of a totally unexpected intervention; she is one of the real Oliver Twists.

And, for that matter, so is Rebecca Jarrett. Turned out to work as a prostitute at the age of 12, Rebecca, like Oliver, was a victim of an economy built on the backs of children. Like Oliver, she was repulsed by the criminal enterprise to which she had been attached as a child. Like Oliver, she repented and threw herself on the kindness of strangers.

Unlike Oliver, Jarrett's conversion to a safe respectability did not proceed in a straight line. She suffered horribly for exposing a sex trafficking industry in London that involved the daily rape of children. But she survived, and she was never tempted to return to a life of crime.

Baby Farming

No examination of the real circumstances that made *Oliver Twist* such an important expose of brutality against children would be complete without at least a brief look at the practice of 'baby farming'.

As an infant, Oliver was farmed out to an auxiliary workhouse which Dickens describes like this:

twenty or thirty other juvenile offenders against the poor-laws rolled about the floor all day, without the inconvenience of too much food or too much clothing, under the parental superintendence of an elderly female, who received the culprits … for the consideration of seven-pence half-penny per small head per week.[12]

This is the Victorian baby farm. Dickens goes on to show that this 'female' keeps most of the money and basically starves the children. Eight out of ten of these children die of 'want', falling into the fire, or being smothered. Dickens's portrayal of the infants as transgressors against the parish and the poor laws ironically underlines the failure of British laws to protect the most innocent and vulnerable members of society.

Baby farms of the Victorian era were not all equally ghastly. Some of them did not passively murder most of the children in their care. But many of them did as the baby farm in *Oliver Twist*. Defying his odds, Oliver somehow survives this institution and, at 9, he ages out of this facility, and goes to the adult workhouse with Mr Bumble.

Dickens's depiction of the baby farms is frighteningly true to historical conditions: the public sporadically expressed concern over the death rate at the local baby farm. But nothing would be done. Surgeons called to investigate a baby's death usually found nothing amiss, and beadles did whatever the parish wanted, which was usually to hush scandal and save money. A board of directors was charged with ensuring the welfare of the farmed babies. In advance of their visits, they sent a beadle to warn the baby farmer who then staged the farm for inspection.

The truth about Victorian baby farms makes the average slasher film seem like a cool breeze on a summer day. But before we dive into that horror, we must first acknowledge that infant mortality at the time was approximately 30 per cent in the first year of life. Family income was an unfortunate, but accurate predictor of infant survival. Poor children died by the droves in and out of baby farms, at a much higher rate than in wealthy or middle-class families.

That said, history has mostly confirmed the truth of what Dickens wrote in *Oliver Twist*: poor children, especially babies, trusted to the care of third parties had poor survival prospects, poorer than average, even after factoring in the income of the parents.

Mr Drouet's Establishment

Ten years after the publication of *Oliver Twist* in book form, Dickens had occasion to speak out against baby farms once more, this time as an editorial writer for the *Examiner*. The case that sparked his outrage was that of Bartholomew Peter Drouet, a baby farmer in Tooting who received 4 shillings and sixpence a week in parish funds for each child in his care.[13] Mr Drouet's Establishment, as it was called, received police and media attention when 180 children in the owner's care died of cholera.

In 1846, Drouet's orphanage held 723 children. Under British law, these children had to have some kind of education, but that was liberally construed. The girls over whom Drouet presided had only seven and a half hours of study a week, and part of that small allotment was spent singing. These same girls, all 14 and under, sewed shirts for four and a half hours a day. Drouet was making money not just on what the parish paid him for board, but also on the products which he forced the children to produce.

By 1848, Drouet's orphanage had expanded, and now there were nearly 1,400 children. The orphanage received warnings and recommendations about the risk of a cholera outbreak two weeks before the children started getting sick. But no particular provisions or sanitary improvements were made to prevent the epidemic from raging through the crowded dorms. In the subsequent investigation, it was noted that no one else in Tooting came down with cholera. Only at the orphanage did it claim victims.

Patrick Sheen, a 10-year-old living at the Drouet orphanage during the cholera outbreak, gave testimony about the children's living conditions. His brief testimony opens a window on a bleak institution

– 'toxic' not just in the sense of unsanitary, but also psychologically abusive. Children were not allowed to take a walk outside because the staff feared they would run away. Despite terrible punishments that ensued, children did often try to run. When they were caught, they were beaten with birch rods and their heads were shaved. Boys who tried to escape were punished by being forced to wear girls' clothing, sometimes for as long as a week.[14]

It came out that the children were underfed, if not starved, and that they lived 200 to a room in unsanitary conditions. Each child had six square feet of living space, substantially less than the space afforded prisoners of the same era.

Before diving into Dickens's coverage of Drouet, we must first acknowledge that the Victorian treatment for cholera was hit or miss. The treatment was, as usual in cases of infection, clean water, nutritious food, and rest in sanitary surroundings, and many patients recovered with this treatment. But the mechanism of fatality in cholera is dehydration. If the patient gets too dehydrated, she dies. In 1883, Dr Thomas Latta published an article on the use of intravenous technology, specifically for use in treating cholera. This technology, which pumps fluids directly into the dehydrated patient, became the first line of defence against cholera fatalities. But Drouet could not have availed himself of this treatment, even if he had meant well by the children in his care.

The doctors and officials who inspected the Drouet orphanage assumed that the cholera was contracted by toxic air, and they noted the poor ventilation and the presence of bad smells. Science has subsequently discovered that cholera can only be contracted by direct contact with infected faecal matter. The most common cause of cholera outbreaks was and still is contaminated water, and contaminated food can also spread the disease through a community.

Therefore, the outbreak of cholera at the baby farm is something of a mystery. If the water had been contaminated, the disease should have killed most of the children. Instead, though the number of victims was high, it was still only a minority percentage of the total population.

One inspection discovered some rotten potatoes, so contaminated food could have been the vector. Another possible vector would have been unsanitary food preparation, i.e. food preparers who passed faecal microbes to the food. And the disease could have been transmitted from one child to another via diarrhoea. The children who contracted cholera frequently soiled their sheets. Where beds were shared and bedding not sterilised, cholera could have spread quickly from one child to the next through contact with bedfellows' waste.

In writing about Drouet, Dickens assumed the same acidic sarcasm that he used to write about the baby farm that Oliver somehow survived. His first article on the Drouet baby farm was titled 'Paradise at Tooting', Tooting being the London district in which the farm was located.

Dickens notes that the deaths at Drouet's orphanage went unexamined in the media and by the magistrates until they reached the attention of Thomas Wakley, a Victorian surgeon, writer, and reformer best known today for founding the *Lancet*. Wakley sounded an alarm about the number of deaths and insisted on a Board of Health investigation. Upon inspection, one Dr Grainger found that the orphanage was poorly ventilated and overcrowded. Their rooms, Dickens wrote, were 'cold, damp, dirty, and rotten'.[15] The children's clothes were dirty and defective. The children were so poorly nourished that they routinely broke into the pigs' pens and stole food from the livestock. And, if they complained, their food rations were cut even more severely. Drouet verbally abused his staff, and allowed the children to be beaten. Drouet and his brother, with whom he ran the business, had taken in far more children than the Board of Health had advised him to take in. But, when it was proposed to remove some of these children for health and safety, Drouet's brother pushed back with threats of violence.

Bartholomew Drouet had a documented history of arguing with people who conducted inspections of his orphanage as a routine part of their jobs. These inspectors described him as behaving violently, accusing them of mistreating him and ruining his 'character'. One group of inspectors abandoned their inspection because Drouet's behaviour toward them was so aggressive. Drouet did not allow children to be interviewed privately. He was always in the room when children were questioned. And if a child complained about the food, Drouet called him a liar and a rascal. Inspectors never followed up on whether children who complained underwent retaliation. Dickens wrote that these wards had learned 'that his precious character – immeasurably more precious than the existence of any number of pauper children – was at stake'.[16]

During the investigation, it emerged that a poor-law inspector had duly visited the Drouets' orphanage and found the children sleeping three to a bed. On follow-up, Drouet claimed he had reduced the number of children per bed to two. However, a new investigation found the children who had contracted cholera sleeping four to a bed.

Dickens's next article on the Drouet farm was titled 'The Tooting Farm'. In this article, our novelist reported that a coroner had dubbed the cholera deaths 'manslaughter' and the case was headed to trial. Dickens here broadened out his condemnation of the cholera deaths in Tooting to include parish authorities who had sent the children to Drouet's orphanage without doing any research into the facility. In fact, children from parishes outside Tooting had been absorbed into Drouet's mega-farm. Dickens, like other reformers of his time, noted how dangerous it was to relocate children. Such relocations invariably separated the children from anyone who might advocate for their care, such as poverty-stricken parents or other family members. Children removed from their home parish were much more vulnerable to mistreatment and starvation.

In 'Tooting Farm', Dickens urges British law to throw the book at Drouet rather than letting sleeping dogs lie, which the author describes as 'that vague disposition to smooth over the things that be'.[17]

Drouet, alone, is not responsible for the deaths of all those children, Dickens implies. There is also the lack of a safety net for poor families. Far too many members of the working poor live in constant danger of delivering their children to the care of the parish:

There are few poor working-men in the kingdom who might not find themselves next year, next month, next week, in the position of those fathers whose children were sent to Tooting; and there are probably very few poor working-men who have not thought 'this might be my child's case, to-morrow.'[18]

Pointing to the Drouet case, Dickens called, unequivocally, for the abolition of baby farms. 'If the system of farming pauper children cannot exist without the danger of another Tooting Farm being weeded by the grisly hands of Want, Disease, and Death, let it now be abolished.'[19] The author also condemned the current poor law and called for it to be reformed or replaced with better legislation.

Though medical experts pronounced Drouet guilty of manslaughter, when his case went to the Central Criminal Court, he was tried only for four deaths. Of those four children, only James Andrews's name survives. Drouet's team mounted an impressive defence. The main point they drove was that the children might have died anyway; it could not be proven that Drouet's neglect had been the decisive factor. Though it could be proven that he had starved the children in his care – some of them had even developed kwashiorkor caused by protein deficiency – it could not be proven that these children had ever been healthy. Judge Baron Platt instructed the jury to find Drouet not guilty, and they obliged. Drouet walked out of court a free man, though he died only a few months later.

Dickens was outraged by the outcome of the trial – and by the trial itself. The defence often scoffed at medical testimony, and the courtroom rang with laughter. The judge sided with the defence early in the trial because he perceived it had the stronger team, Dickens believed.

Dark as were Dickens's fictional and non-fiction depictions of baby farms, he did not capture all the worst aspects of these facilities. Opium overdoses were a common murder weapon used against children. Victorian law allowed the use of opium (packaged as laudanum) on babies, so if a baby screamed, she could be dosed. Overdoses were rarely prosecuted as murder, but treated as inevitable.

Another, less obvious manslaughter weapon was to make 'milk' out of cornstarch (then called 'cornflower') and water and serve this to children because it was cheaper than mammal milk. Of course, the cornstarch concoction did not contain enough protein to ensure that a baby would thrive. It seems likely that at least some of the women who served this 'milk' to babies did so out of ignorance and not as a deliberate attempt to kill the infant.

Almost every institution in England in some way colluded in the murder of babies on baby farms, as Dickens aptly describes. The parish leaders didn't want the cost of living babies, the parents – often unwed mothers and unidentifiable fathers – didn't want the cost of living babies, the doctors did not want to bring charges against paying clients, the nurses who cared for the babies did not want to spend their profit margin on feeding babies.

The farm system that raised Oliver from birth to the age of 9 was not the worst of the baby farms, mainly because the manager received a weekly stipend to care for the children. Another, quite a bit more sinister, practice of lump payments was also allowed. Parents, usually unwed mothers, could advertise their babies for adoption and pay the adopter a lump sum for the care of the child. That sum was never enough to cover the true costs of raising an infant, even to the age of 8, at which time a child could be forced to work and earn money. The adopter, who was typically in it for the quick cash, had every motivation to let the baby die, either by neglect or by opium.

On first review, it is easy to condemn the women who left their babies with a baby farmer. Surely they knew that the child was likely to die via neglect or murder. Some mothers may have passively collaborated in the killing of their sons and daughters, but other mothers went to heroic lengths to keep their children fed and cared for. In the *Seven Curses of London*, James Greenwood cites the example of a young woman who worked in the manufacture of paper bags. She never made more than 6 shillings and threepence a week; out of that, she paid her baby farmer 4 shillings and sixpence. That left 1 shilling and nine pennies for the mother's own upkeep. Despite that sacrifice, the baby farmer got drunk one night and left the baby exposed to the winter air. The infant died.[20]

The Failure of Charity

When it came to caring for an illegitimate child, mothers had no good choices. In a better world, such a woman could rely on public aid to raise her child; however, such aid was not forthcoming in the nineteenth century. For most unwed mothers, the best-case scenario was placement in a charitable institution with a good reputation. However, a look at London's Foundling Hospital quickly shows how selective such an institution could be.

The Foundling Hospital was founded in 1739 by philanthropist Thomas Coram. Though it was called a hospital, it was an orphanage. For years, the policy of this institution was to take in all abandoned children. When this became impossible, because of a huge influx of babies from all over the United Kingdom, the hospital restricted admission to children who came attached to large sums of money, typically £100.

By 1801, this obviously vile practice had been discontinued. But there were still far more children born out of wedlock than the hospital could accommodate. Furthermore, this foundling hospital was known to be the gold standard for raising illegitimate children. It was aggressive in its efforts to maintain hygiene and stop the spread of diseases. It was well endowed by rich philanthropists. The famed composer George Frideric Handel had even given a concert there in 1749. So, naturally, unwed mothers effectively queued up to get their children into this place.

A merit system was adopted. All mothers who wished to place their babies with the hospital were unwed, but the hospital staff established a protocol to determine the relative virtue of these mothers. The child had to be the result of a first and isolated incident of sexual misconduct; no children of prostitutes were accepted. It occurred to no one that the offspring of prostitutes might have the greater need or that the need of the child should be the main concern here.

Women who had their babies accepted by the hospital had to pass an interview. 'In front of a panel of middle-aged and elderly men, the young women were forced to describe the details of their sex lives, and their sexual history.'[21] If a young mother could convince this board of review that she had been raped or seduced by an employer, her child was much more likely to be accepted. If she had considered suicide to circumvent her shame, so much the better. The mother's interview started when the porter admitted her to the hospital and made notes about her appearance, especially how she was dressed.

As we now know, however, even very sexually active women with multiple partners love their babies. These more sexually experienced women were reduced to lying about how their child was conceived. In her interview, Ann Gidding claimed she had become pregnant with the footman's child while a servant at a respectable home. Upon investigation, her employer and employer's address turned out to have been fabricated, and her application was denied. 'They knew what they had to say to get their baby saved, and it was that they had been respectable, that they had fallen from virtue, and that they could return to respectability if they could give up their babies,'[22] writes Joanna Moorhead of the *Guardian*.

At the end of the day, the Foundling Hospital could only take so many babies. Meanwhile, the unwed mothers themselves could not provide for their own children because they could not get jobs. The stigma of having an illegitimate child was such that a woman couldn't even get or keep a job as a barmaid if she was known to have a child out of wedlock.

Margaret Waters

Greed and indifference are by no means an invention of the twentieth or twenty-first century. Today, taxpayers often begrudge payments to maintain the children of poor women. The nineteenth century was no more generous. And, at that time, there was simply no system of public aid for unmarried mothers and their children. Barred from both employment *and* public aid, mothers of unwanted children were in a desperate position. The men who had impregnated them routinely recommended suicide, and the charities that would take a baby and raise it kindly were few, far between, and sorely oversubscribed. This was the system that produced baby farmer Margaret Waters.

Born in 1835, in Brixton, Waters led a conventional life – until she was 28, when she became a widow. She had £500 in savings when her husband died, but she made the mistake of starting up a clothing factory and lost all her money when her business could not compete with larger corporations making cheaper clothes. Waters then rented rooms, but found that the rent she received was still less than the rent she owed. Within years of her husband's death, she was deeply in debt and on the precipice of living in the street.

She took up baby farming some time in 1866, as a way of making a living, along with her sister, Sara Ellis. She seems to have come into the trade by chance. One of her tenants, pregnant and unwed, gave Margaret £3 to take charge of her baby. Margaret accepted the baby and the money. Then, she successfully placed the infant in the home of a wealthy family who paid her £9. It seems likely that Waters hoped to repeat this success when she placed numerous advertisements in the local newspaper, asking for babies for adoption.

At this point, historians diverge over whether or not the Waters sisters were cold-blooded killers or just really unlucky and poorly educated childcare providers. By some estimates nineteen children died under Margaret's care. She stands accused of drugging the babies in her care and starving them. She wrapped the dead bodies and left them in the streets. Michael Newton placed her in his *Encyclopedia of Serial Killers*, published in 2006. And Madame Tussaud's Wax Museum featured a wax effigy of Margaret Waters until sometime in the 1970s.

However, historian Katherine Field has published a much more sympathetic account of Margaret Waters's activity, an account that paints Waters herself as a victim of a ruthless society. Like the unwed mothers whose infants she accepted, Waters had no skills except sewing, no ability to find well-paid work, no real business savvy, and failing prospects.

Field notes that illegitimate babies were twice as likely as legitimate babies to die before reaching one year of age. She blames this on the absence of mother's breast milk, but the sad truth is that the illegitimacy of the babies was probably the greater danger to their lives. Some unwed mothers did kill their own children; otherwise, workhouses and baby farmers gave babies indifferent care and spared a great deal of expense in feeding them and providing medical care.

Many of the children in Waters's care had diarrhoea which, Field posits, was secondary to dehydration, occurring in the absence of frequent breastfeeding. It is puzzling that, during the investigation into her 'murders', Waters produced receipts for real milk and for medical care. John Walter Cowen, the infant whose death prompted a police investigation, had been taken to a doctor. Cowen's grandfather had placed John in Waters's care when his unmarried daughter gave birth to a child. For whatever reason, police became interested in what had happened to John Walter Cowen and they traced him to Waters's quarters.

In the ensuing trial, the media often demonised Waters as a monster. The public's thirst for her execution may have driven her death sentence. Waters's brothers were joined by several MPs in asking that her hanging be commuted. Even three jurors who sat on Waters's trial asked that her sentence be reduced to manslaughter. But the public and the media were keen for Waters to be an unmitigated villain, and villains must hang. Her sister received eighteen months of hard labour.

'It is ironic Waters was executed for the murder of a child society did not otherwise value,' Field notes.

Margaret Waters's main contribution to society was to spur a spate of articles in the media of the day about baby farming. Of course, most of these articles affirmed that women should stay virgins until married and that baby farmers were monsters. Few, if any, of these publications looked at the larger issues that surrounded the problem of babies who were unwanted because they were not born within wedlock. The atrocious education Victorian girls received at almost every level of society, the lack of work opportunities for women, the injustice of stigmatising a child for something far beyond his control – none of these issues made it into the newspapers following Margaret Waters's trial.

In 1870, an unsigned article in the *Spectator* articulated the Victorian concern that, if illegitimate children received public aid, it would encourage 'immorality,' i.e. women would be more prone to have unsanctioned sex. 'The state cannot be mother to all children their parents wish to get rid of, for if it were … the number of such children would be multiplied.'[23] Women with unplanned babies, therefore, were driven to baby farms, and these businesses were conducted in the broad light of day with the collusion of polite society.

In examining the problem of murders on baby farms, the *Spectator* article suggests, tepidly, that lump sum payments could be outlawed. But the need to shame unwed mothers is the article's primary purpose, and it pervades the entire article. Any solution must not increase 'the temptation … to unchastity'.[24] The mothers of illegitimate children must be 'punished' somehow. At one point, the author suggests that infanticide be decriminalised, implying that it is somehow better for a mother to kill her own child than to hire someone else to do it. Desperate mothers, who kill their own babies, are mostly 'escaping torture or hoping heaven for the child'.[25] The best solution to baby farming, as the *Spectator* author sees it, is to replace baby farms with private charities whose doings are well documented and who extract weekly payment from the mothers: 'A charity which made the mother pay a weekly fee … might, we imagine, suppress child murder without diminishing unduly the woman's terror of any departure from a chaste life.'[26]

Also in 1870, the *British Controversialist* published a pro/con article that explored the question, 'Ought baby-farming to be prohibited?' The article is in two parts, and presumably written by two different unnamed authors. The first part argues for making such care facilities illegal. This argument again blames unwed mothers for creating the problem in the first place. Baby farms, the unnamed author argues, give the green light to a loss of virtue:

> The knowledge that infants can be easily disposed of at a baby-farm is calculated to make persons of a certain disposition careless as to the commission of the sin of fornication, an evil which is now so rampant as to call for every possible check to be put upon it.[27]

One of those checks should definitely be the cost and difficulty of raising an unwanted child, the author goes on to say: 'The fact that baby-farming holds out a hope to evil doers that the licentiousness which they have committed will be concealed, is itself a premium upon wickedness.'[28]

The *British Controversialist*'s editors most likely thought that baby farming should *not* be outlawed. The reader can deduce this from the weakness of the pro-outlawing essay and the relative superiority of the following argument against outlawing the farms. There will always be a percentage of dead mothers, the writer argues, so baby farming cannot be outlawed.

From this historical distance, it is obvious that the best way to eliminate baby farms was to empower single mothers, creating laws that prohibited employers from discriminating against them on the basis of procreation. But the 1870 *British Controversialist* coverage fails to consider that aspect. Instead, that publication did as its peers in publishing did: it further demonised single mothers.

The *Times* published a similar article which concluded that many baby farms were committing nothing short of murder. As a result of these outcries, the Infant Life Protection Act was passed by Parliament in 1872. The act merely required baby farms to be registered, however, and it cannot be documented that the act substantially reduced the number of infant deaths caused as a result of the baby farm system. In fact, the most publicised examples of baby farm death occurred after the passage of this act which did not limit the number of babies a farmer could take into care.

Betty Binmore

The abysmal failure of the Infant Life Protection Act can immediately be documented in the case of Betty Binmore of Newton. Binmore took in babies without registering her business, as the act required. For years, however, police showed no interest in her operation. At least four of the babies she 'cared' for died before her farm was investigated in 1875.

Binmore seems to have brought the investigation upon herself when she reported to local law enforcement personnel that one of her babies, Margaret Phillips, had died. This led police to the children she still had alive in her care who were found to be severely emaciated. Margaret's mother, Mary Phillips, had given birth to Margaret in a workhouse five months earlier, in 1874.

Mary had been paying Binmore 2 shillings and sixpence a week for the care of her baby. Interestingly, another 1 shilling and sixpence was paid, weekly, by a board of guardians for the child's care. Obviously, the parish which provided this money was not following up very closely, either on adherence to the Infant Life Protection Act or on whether the children were adequately cared for.

Betty Binmore's trial uncovered a network of negligent practitioners. Binmore had duly taken Margaret to several doctors prior to the infant's death, but none of them would examine or diagnose the child without payment. And payment was not forthcoming. A chemist sold Binmore a medicinal powder that was supposed to make Margaret better, but the baby got worse.

Binmore maintained a 'bread book' that showed a record of feeding the children, and this was produced during her investigation and subsequent trial. It emerged that the 'milk' Binmore had been feeding her wards was a non-nutritive mixture of cornstarch and water. Such a diet would explain the babies' malnutrition, even if the portions had been generous. But only after Margaret's death did one of the local doctors explain to Binmore that the cornstarch and water solution was insufficient nutrition for a growing baby.

Though the doctors who refused treatment were not charged with crimes, the trial proceedings did criticise them for prioritising payment over the baby's life. Trial documents also note that the police should have investigated an unregistered baby farm and that the guardians should have known that 1 shilling and sixpence was not enough to raise a child. During the trial, it further emerged that there was a parish 'relieving officer' whose job should have encompassed paying a doctor to examine the baby.

Betty Binmore's story is troubling, because she may have been guided by ignorance more than malice. She did not take lump sum payments, and the money she received from the board of guardians should have ensured some oversight, but did not. The magistrates who tried the case bumped her sentence down from murder to manslaughter for obvious reasons. If the board of guardians was not enforcing the Infant Life Protection Act, how could anyone expect a woman like Betty Binmore to understand that she had to register her business? When doctors withheld life-saving information about baby nutrition, how was she to understand that cornstarch is not an adequate replacement for milk?

For these reasons, Binmore served twelve years in prison instead of hanging. She survived her sentence and died at the age of 80, having worked as a charwoman in her 70s.

Amelia Dyer

Amelia Dyer is arguably the most famous of the criminal baby farmers. Dyer began her career in 'childcare' in 1869, just before the passage of the Infant Life Protection Act. In her first years as a baby farmer, she may or may not have practised the same shadow murder as others in her profession. Several babies died while under her alleged protection, and a trial followed an investigation. She was charged with neglect leading to the infant deaths and served six months' hard labour. The historical record strongly suggests that she developed mental illness during her imprisonment. History has played down the obvious role of psychosis in Dyer's subsequent actions.

Upon her release from prison, she went straight back to farming babies. But shortly after her incarceration, she started murdering them more directly. In at least two murders, she used a fabric tape to strangle the children. She tied the tape around the babies' necks and let them suffocate. When she was finally apprehended, she admitted that she had enjoyed watching the children perish. Clearly, Dyer's mental illness had not been thoroughly examined or properly diagnosed during her first trial or prison sentence.

She was finally brought to justice when someone fished a baby's body out of the Thames where Dyer had dumped it. Police raided her home and did not find any bodies, but the smell of human remains was pervasive. They found enough circumstantial evidence to bring Dyer to trial: fabric tape, communications from parents looking to farm their babies and children, and, heartbreakingly, letters from parents who had hired Dyer inquiring about the welfare of their children.

Not every mother who passed a baby to Dyer had passively consented in the murder of her child. Evelina Marmon had an illegitimate baby, named Doris, at the age of 25. Marmon was employed as a barmaid, and she had hoped to retrieve her child from Dyer, presumably at a point when she could provide for Doris.

Marmon intuited that baby farmers who took periodic payments were a safer bet for ensuring the welfare of her child. And she proposed such a payment system. But Dyer insisted on an upfront lump sum payment. Evelina accepted these terms, moved by Dyer's declarations that she had no child of her own and loved children. Evelina raised the requested £10. Doris was promptly strangled with fabric tape, and Evelina received her baby's remains after she was fished from the Thames.

Dyer was found guilty of murder and hanged. As such, she became the fourth of eight baby farmers who would be sentenced to capital punishment and executed in Britain. Considering how rampant infant mortality was among the baby farmers, it seems like a low number. And, at the same time, one wonders if the hanged baby farmers were not scapegoated for a systemic problem in which most legitimate elements of society conspired.

Chapter 6

George Elson and the Climbing Boys

In the musical *Oliver!*, Bumble takes Oliver into the street and tries to sell him. The haunting tune, 'One boy, boy for sale', forms the soundtrack to this pathos. As one scene gives way to the next, Oliver's price goes down from 7 guineas to £3 10 shillings.

The reality for workhouse children was not that simple. They were not actually sold. They were 'indentured'. To the modern conscience, Victorian indenture and child trafficking look very similar. The workhouse beadle found someone to take a child off his hands and paid that person a small sum with the promise that the boy would be taught a skill and fed and housed. The only failsafe, and it was not really a failsafe at all, was that a magistrate had to sign off on the apprenticeship. Magistrates were, ostensibly, responsible for making decisions that were in the interests of these orphan children. But, in reality, they often just wanted to save the parish money by unloading charity children as quickly and cheaply as possible.

There was rarely any follow-up to ensure the safety of the child. As we have seen in the example of Robert Blincoe, this system led to terrible abuses. If employers had been obliged to buy their apprentices, they might have treated them better. As it stood, an unscrupulous 'boss' could accept payment for indenturing a child, then disappear, leaving that boy to fend for himself.

Potentially the worst form of Victorian indenture was chimney sweeping. In *Oliver Twist*, Oliver narrowly escapes the fate of a sweep. Before taking Oliver to the magistrate, Bumble, the workhouse tyrant, instructs Oliver to put on a happy face and say that he wants to be a chimney sweep. Oliver bursts into tears, as he so frequently does, so Bumble hammers him with the amount that the parish is paying for this indentureship.

The magistrate is mostly blind and senile, but he does go through a few of the expected motions. He asks Oliver if he wishes to be indentured as a sweep. Bumble quickly answers for him, with typical florid exaggeration: 'He dotes on it, your worship ... If we was to bind him to any other trade to-morrow, he'd run away simultaneous.'[1] Mr Gamfield, the master sweep, promises that he will care for Oliver. The magistrate is half an inch away from signing Oliver's fate when he gets a good look at the child's horrified face. Oliver bursts into tears (again), and prays to be spared. Beat him, kill him, he says. He would rather die than go with Gamfield. The magistrate declines to sign the papers and tells the beadle to take Oliver back to the workhouse and 'treat him kindly'.[2]

Interestingly, it's not the work that Oliver is scared of. He has too little knowledge of the sweep's trade to understand its dangers. Oliver is terrified of Gamfield because his 'villainous countenance was a regular stamped receipt for cruelty'.[3]

In creating Gamfield, it seems likely that Dickens had in mind some of the highly publicised cruelty toward chimney sweeps that had made memorable headlines. In the years that Dickens began his work as a novelist, the deaths of so-called 'climbing boys' had forced the nation to recognise the problem of child labour, even if only for moments at a time. In 1822, 9-year-old Valentine Grey was murdered by his 'master', Benjamin Davies, on the Isle of Wight. An inquest revealed the cause of death to be a hard blow to the head. However, there were bruises and other wounds all over the dead boy's body, strongly suggesting that he had been beaten, repeatedly, over many weeks.

Like Oliver, Valentine was an orphan whose mother died when he was six months old. So he fell to the mercy of poor house administration, like Twist and like Blincoe. He was placed in Alverstoke workhouse where he was one of 122 children. There he was adequately fed and clothed. But, as we know, workhouse administrations were eager to offload their children, at obscenely young ages, in order to lessen the tax burden on their parishes. Valentine was therefore apprenticed to

Davies at the age of 8 or 9, in 1821. Under Davies's chaperonage, the child made the boat trip to the Isle of Wight.

According to Isle of Wight historian Roger Fruen, Valentine's body was found at the Rum Puncheon, a public house and house of prostitution in Newport. As a chimney sweep, Valentine would have been required to climb chimneys as narrow as twelve inches, and he climbed naked, presumably because there was no room for clothes or because his employer was a sadist. In the course of his work, he would get scratched, and the scratches would immediately make contact with chimney soot, making infection inevitable and healing slow. This, however, was just business as usual for the smallest chimney sweeps.

What shocked the newspaper-reading public were the needless cruelties that Valentine suffered, at the hands of a master who, no doubt, had some kind of mental illness. Numerous witnesses came forward at Davies's trial. They had seen Valentine tied to a chair, beaten, and whipped. Davies had thrown water at his apprentice's naked body. Davies was found guilty of murder, but he served no time in prison. His sentence was merely to pay a fine of 1 shilling, worth approximately £5 in today's money.

In the story of Valentine Grey, we again see the dangers of sending workhouse children to remote locations. The further a child went from his place of origin, or at least from a responsible workhouse, the less accountability there was for his welfare. Though Alverstoke is not that far from Newport, the fact of taking his apprentice across to an island no doubt gave Davies a sense that he could abuse his apprentice with impunity.

The torture and death of Valentine Grey was not unique. Master Chimney Sweeper J. Hogarth flew into a rage with one of his sweeps and lit a fire under the boy in order to force him to come down. The unnamed sweep was hiding out from his master because a brush had become stuck in the flue. Perhaps rightly, the apprentice sweep believed he would be blamed and beaten for the lost brush. When he felt the flames lit under him, in an unreasoned panic, he climbed higher. It appears he got stuck and suffocated to death. Another sweep went up to recover him, but could not. Eventually, the chimney had to be dismantled, but the boy was already dead.

Like Davies, Hogarth was tried and similarly found guilty. There was some discussion of serving a prison sentence, but his sentence was commuted when one or more doctors declared that the boy died of suffocation.

These were the stories uppermost in Dickens's mind when he created the character of Gamfield. Into Oliver's face, the novelist wrote all the horror of the boys who had died at the hands of cruel masters, after being squeezed into airless brick passageways, beaten, burned, and waterboarded. Dickens had already determined to give Oliver a happy ending, and it appears the novelist could not see a way to do that, if Oliver were to become a chimney sweep.

To give Parliament credit where at least some credit is due, that body did pass numerous laws attempting to curb the abuse and murder of small children for the sake of clean chimneys. A 1788 act, the Act For the Better Regulation of Chimney Sweepers and their Apprentices, set the minimum age of sending a child up a chimney at 8.

In 1834, after the murder of 10-year-old Valentine Grey, another law was passed raising the minimum age of the climbing boy to 10. Dickens may have intended to show just how easy it was to bypass these parliamentary acts when he nearly apprenticed Oliver to a master sweeper at the age of 9.

Through his brief but powerful suggestion that apprenticing children as sweeps was tantamount to murder, Dickens may have influenced the next law, the Chimney Sweepers Regulation Act of 1840. This law forbade apprenticing anyone under 16 as a chimney sweep, and it also specified that no one under 21 could be compelled to climb a chimney.

The problem with these laws was the difficulty of enforcing them. While there *were* relatively well-off master chimney sweepers with multiple cared-for apprentices, living in the broad light of day, many master sweeps were sole proprietors, with only one climbing boy, irregular schedules, no fixed abode, and rotating customers.

Such sweeps illustrate how poverty is self-perpetuating. The poorest sweeps served the poorest neighbourhoods. The houses there would have had the worst chimneys, poorly built, jagged, and filled with the worst soot.

As Benita Cullingford explains, the poor of England could not afford to burn hardwood, which burned clean and left less debris behind in the burning. That left the poorer citizens burning 'faggots', i.e. sticks bundled together to create a makeshift log, coal, and vegetable peelings, especially potato. These peelings would be put at the back of the fire to dry them, then they were added to the coal or sticks to create a composite fuel. This part-vegetable fuel left behind a thick, heavy soot that was time consuming to clean: 'It burned like pitch and blackened the chimney top. Chimney sweeps often removed encrustations an inch thick from the sides of the flue,' Cullingford writes.[4] The owners and renters of these chimneys would have less money to pay for chimney cleaning. The Gamfields of the Victorian era would send their apprentices up these toxic flues to spend hours scraping the debris off the walls.

The poorer master sweep typically rented two rooms, one of which he lived in with his wife if he had one. The second room, always the poorer, maybe an attic, would be used for storing soot, brushes, and housing the apprentice. This boy or girl would usually sleep on straw or even a bag of soot.[5]

Chimney sweeping, especially for the poor practitioner, was seasonal work that had to be supplemented with other work. The most common side gig for a chimney sweep and his apprentice was euphemistically called 'night soil'. This was the work of removing human waste out of the latrines, privies, middens, or anywhere else it gathered and carting it away. This work was, by necessity, carried out at night when respectable humanity was sleeping. Night soil removal was one more way that master chimney sweeps stayed out of the public eye.

It was difficult to enforce a parliamentary act on the poor master sweep and his poorer apprentice who lived so far out of range of the hawkish middle-class eye. If workhouses and magistrates actually did their jobs and prevented underage children from being deliberately engaged to climb chimneys, there were other methods of getting around the law. Many apprenticeships were informal, i.e. illegal. The most obvious way around the law was simply to buy a child from its parents. Some Victorian families were so poor that they would give their children to chimney sweepers at no charge, just to shake off the financial burden of a child.

Even people who were aware of the laws, or should have been, were generally free to flout them at will. Workhouses could pretend not even to know the birth year of a child, and if the child's age was not an issue for the workhouse, the master, or the magistrate who signed indentures, the child had little to no recourse.

The failure of Parliament to prevent children from dying in chimneys is nowhere better illustrated than in the death of George Brewster in 1875. His master, William Wyer, sent him up the chimney of Fulbourn Hospital where Brewster got stuck. A wall was removed in an attempt to save him, but he died within hours of being removed from the chimney. The doctor who treated him found his mouth filled with soot. Sources differ on the age of Brewster at the time of his death, but several say he was 11. Because he was in such clear and public violation of the 1840 chimney sweep act, Wyer was found guilty of manslaughter.[6]

Brewster was the last climbing boy that we know of to die in one of England's chimneys. In the wake of Brewster's death, Parliament passed another act, this one called the Chimney Sweepers Act of 1875. Championed by the Earl of Shaftesbury, the new act did have the virtue of requiring chimney sweeps to register with the police and undergo supervision. For that reason, many people credit the 1875 act with ending the cycle of dead climbing boys. But it seems much more likely that compulsory education was the deciding factor in preventing children from dying in chimneys.

Out of the gloom of the chimney sweeping underworld blossoms the story of George Elson, chimney sweep, writer, and holistic medicine man. George began climbing chimneys around the age of 10 in 1840, just when the law decided he shouldn't be doing that work for another six years. We have the details of Elson's life because he published his autobiography in 1900. Elson's writing seems deliberately to imitate the bright, wide-eyed buoyancy of Charles Dickens. The reader often suspects him of glossing over unpleasant subjects, such as why he ran away from home at 10.

Elson was born into the middle class, the indelible mark of which was the existence of a servant who minded him when his parents were away. His mother and father were 'hawkers', i.e. travelling fabric salesmen. Their work week consisted of journeying to a market town, establishing a base at an inn, then moving around the countryside, door to door, selling their fabrics. Elson represents them as honest tradesmen who sold quality goods that stood up well to scrutiny from multiple female householders prior to purchase.

Elson's memoir is often short on exact details, especially years, but it appears he did learn to read at a very young age. That was lucky, because the death of his father plunged his family into poverty, and he would never recover the luxury of a formal education. His father was a drinker. Elson describes him, with perhaps excessive charity, as a man who liked to have a good time a little too often: 'The too frequent celebration of success in a multitude of liquors strong, combined with a reckless indulgence in physical feats, proved, however, the means of hastening the end of an otherwise unblemished career...'[7]

After his father's death, Elson's mother gave birth to a fourth child. Try as she might, she could not keep her family out of the workhouse. The poor laws of the time allowed one workhouse to transfer them to another, and they ended up in the Lutterworth Union, Leicestershire workhouse in the parish where Elson's grandfather had been apprenticed.

The boy was briefly reprieved from the workhouse by an aunt and uncle. When these relatives sent him back to the workhouse, he chalked it up to their inability to get along with each other. Again, one suspects Elson of reaching hard for an optimistic construction on things. The source of his aunt and uncle's difficulties was, repetitively, the uncle's love of an alcoholic beverage. But children can find beauty in a sordid situation. He remembered, with great fondness, his uncle's musical talent and the barn dances that he went to with that relative.

Elson's grandparents were the next family members to remove him from the workhouse, and he writes fondly of them, as he does of almost everyone. Like his father, these grandparents were hawkers. Released from the workhouse, Elson travelled with them and admired the views of Bedfordshire. During this time, he regretted that he was unable to continue his education. He scrounged free newspapers from public houses, and asked to borrow books. Somehow he was able to improve his mind with a few classics: *Robinson Crusoe*, *Pilgrim's Progress*, *Bruce*, *Wallace*, and, of course, the family Bible, which he resorted to when nothing else was available. Unaccountably, his grandfather owned a book about the serial wife killer, Bluebeard, and asked for it to be read aloud to him on occasion. In Elson's determination to find and read books of some calibre, we can see his yearning for a more thorough education than what fate handed him, and in this, he is similar to Dickens. His tireless pursuit of a fine-tuned literacy would enable him to write an entertaining and informative memoir half a century later.

He depicts his time with his grandparents as a pleasant interlude. However, when a brother showed up and said that his mother was remarried and out of the workhouse, Elson wished to rejoin her and his siblings. So he did. Elson's new father was also a travelling salesman, one who dealt in pottery, mostly. Elson represents him as a man of few words, but kind enough. But there are signs that this newly reconfigured family is not as well off as the original. There is no servant to hold things down at home. The children often travel with their stepfather and mother on their sales jaunts. They camp out to save money on lodging.

Charmingly, Elson never indicates that strained finances were his reason for running away – the first time. He characterises his first attempt to leave home as the childish fancy of a boy with no good sense. He was 10 at the time, and he took his 7-year-old brother with him. They survived for a couple days on the sale of some haberdashery with which they had been trusted, but they were soon sleeping on the grass with no resources and no plan of action. A compassionate police officer found them sleeping rough, and they were sent to a workhouse while their parents were located, which took several months. Charitable institutions differ widely in their treatment of their clients; this workhouse was superior to many. Elson was well treated, and he even received some education which he greatly valued. When his parents finally came for him, they treated him with the same kindness they had applied before.

After that, the family soon fell into true destitution, due to bad weather that made travelling impossible. This time, Elson left with a brother who was three years his senior. Their main forms of income for the next weeks were begging and scavenging. They fell in with some entertainers and accompanied them to the Coventry Fair. Elson and his brother tried to learn acrobatics. For a very short time, their clumsiness was amusing to the troupe and their audience, but soon the professionals wanted to part ways and gave the boys a few 'coppers'. The brothers combed the fair, alternately scrounging scraps of food and being mesmerised by the acts.

They found a hovel to sleep in, but even this free lodging already had customers. The prior residents were criminals, boys, of course, and they tried to lure Elson and his brother to join them. The Elsons were young and innocent looking, these already jaded boys thought, and it would be easy for them to pick pockets. There would be no occasion to test this theory. The Elsons awoke to find the other boys being arrested. Here Elson, the writer, sees an opportunity to boost his similarity to a Dickens character. Like Oliver, he had no vocation for crime. 'Although destitute, starving and wretched, neither of us felt the slightest inclination to turn thieves.'[8]

The brothers wound their way to Northampton where they had various family members. It turned out that their grandparents were away, but an aunt wished them to stay and gave them money for lodging. They had difficulty finding a respectable place to stay, however. At the rental accommodations available, the condition of the rooms and the low character of the residents were bad enough to drive them outdoors, again, to sleep. The Elsons thought they had found the solution when they spied a giant, flaming brick kiln out in the fields. This, they thought, would provide plenty of warmth for al fresco sleeping. They fashioned beds out of 'hurdles' and blankets of some loose organic matter that was on the ground. They woke to find their makeshift blankets aflame, and the hurdles quickly followed.

From there, the Elsons made their way to Boughton Green Fair, where the main attraction was a maze. The brothers mastered the maze quickly and were able to make some money leading less astute customers through it.

By this time, the rough sleeping and failure to launder their clothes or buy new ones had taken their toll on the boys' appearance. They found begging much harder than formerly. They had lost the look of injured innocence on which they had traded easily at the beginning. Now, people loosed their dogs on the two, and the Elsons had to use sticks and kicks to keep themselves from being bitten. They had to be careful where they lay down at night. Barns were not safe because they were often rat infested. George became so malnourished at one point that he fell to the ground, unable to keep moving. He was rescued by some villagers who fed and watered him back to health.

They found work haymaking, and that sustained them for a while, but it was seasonal work. When the season ran its course, they hit the road again. A few miles outside Newark, the brothers met a friendly master sweep who treated them to ale and let them sleep in the stables with his climbing boys. George and Charlie were initiated into chimney sweeping, literally in their sleep. They woke up to find themselves and their clothes covered in soot. The cause turned out to be the blanket that the master sweep had laid over them while they were fast asleep. It was filthy, having been used to capture chimney soot for who knows how long. George implies that the master sweep deliberately made them so dirty that they were fit for no other work but cleaning chimneys. He describes it, from the outset, as a 'dark and dismal trade'.[9]

Looking back on his life as an adult, Elson brings the knowledge of the chimney sweep act of 1840 to his story. By the 1840s, machines had been invented that could clean chimneys without endangering children. Those machines may have effected some humanitarian improvements in London, he speculated, but in more rural areas, children were still used as sweeps with impunity, and the householders who had to pay for clean chimneys conspired to let the practice continue. 'Thus it was rendered possible for me and other boys, without fear of prosecution, to climb chimneys anywhere, in defiance of the majestic laws of Great Britain.'[10]

Almost immediately, the brothers were separated. Their 'master' sent Charlie, the elder, to Lincoln to live with and learn the trade from another master sweep. George climbed his first chimney in Long Bennington. Luckily, it was straight and represented no unusual challenges. He quickly learned the knack of climbing by applying pressure to the walls of the chimney with his knees, feet, hands, and elbows. He rose to the top, scraped, and came down with no difficulty. For this, he received twopence.

He quickly learned the daily occupational hazard of the trade: his face stung from contact with soot, and he had to keep bathing it in cold water to ease the discomfort. Over the next few days, his knees and elbows would become scraped and infected, and this cycle would continue until permanent scar tissue, the size and shape of shillings, formed over his climbing limbs.

George also learned the purpose of the 'climbing cap', a cap made of coarse cloth (unbleached calico in George's case) that the sweeps pulled all the way over their faces and tucked in at the neck while climbing. It was basically like putting one's head in a canvas bag. This was meant to protect the climbers from absorbing too much soot through their noses and mouths. Unfortunately, it made breathing in tight, airless spaces even more of a challenge. And George noted that it did not make a perfect barrier; he still breathed soot in.

He frequently found himself climbing chimneys in which the fires had only just been put out. The stone was still hot, breathing was even more difficult, and sulphurous fumes still lingered from the recent fire. Decaying plaster was yet another hazardous inhalant. On more than one occasion, he passed out from the fumes and fell from high up in the shaft. Chunks of brick and mortar frequently broke off and hit him on the head. Many shafts were so narrow that his trouser pockets filled up with soot as he climbed. On many occasions, he had to take his trousers off and drop them down the chute ahead of his descent. Otherwise, they might have caused him to get stuck on his way down. During this time in Elson's life, a straight, cool chimney was a godsend. But irregular chimneys were the norm. In one house where he worked, a single shaft served three different fires. Knowing which one to descend became a challenge.

Nevertheless, George was good at this work. He climbed with dexterity, never panicked, used good technique, and kept his sense of humour. Most importantly, he never made the chimney sweep's fatal error of letting his knees go too high. For safety, knees always had to be kept well below the waist. If this safety measure were flouted, the sweep could end up jammed in the chimney, unable to go up or down. First another boy would be sent up to pull him. If that didn't work, they used ropes, but sometimes a boy got so badly jammed in the chimney, a stone mason had to tear up part of the brickwork. Children did not always survive that process. Amidst the suffocation, the panic, and the fumes, they were frequently removed as corpses.

Another immediate danger to the sweeping child was the chimney fire. This is not what it sounds like. Chimney fires did not start in the fireplace, they started higher in the chimney. Therefore, they could not just be put out with a bucket of water. These spontaneously erupting fires were usually caused by an excess of soot build up. A drifting spark, a sizzle of uncontained cooking oil could start up one of these fires, and they were dangerous. They could burn down the whole house. In some villages, whole rows of cottages were lost due to chimney fires. And such fires were elusive; sometimes, the homeowners would think the fire was gone, but it would remain hidden in a crook of the chimney, unnoticed until the walls started sweating.

George had to face down his share of chimney fires. He believed that, when confronted with an unknown fire, his best course of action was to keep ascending and put the fire out as best he could on the way to the roof.

George always felt, like Dickens and Blincoe, that he was born for something better. But the buoyancy of his nature did not allow him to wallow in self-pity. He and his fellow sweeps learned how to make a game of it. When two chimneys in nearby houses ran parallel, they held races to see who could climb to the top fastest. He found it amusing when a chimney rocked under his weight. Like other people on whom sorrow finds it difficult to stick, he sang while working. He competed with his peers for best climber and bravely learned to ascend chimneys that were no wider than nine inches on all four sides.

He quickly discovered that chimney cleaning is seasonal. In nice weather, people didn't use fires, and chimney maintenance would be deferred. Elson describes a short season that he spent bringing in the harvest as a very happy memory. He enjoyed the company of fifty or so assembled farm workers who worked and dined together. The work was relatively light because so many people joined together, they ate well, usually at picnics, there was plenty of ale, and they liked to burst into song. The sunny nature of this agrarian life contrasts with the cold, dark work which was Elson's lot the rest of the year.

With Newark as their base, the sweeps travelled miles out into the countryside, often without enough warm clothes, sometimes with a donkey, but largely on foot. The day began at three or four in the morning. They relied on their clients to feed them breakfast, which meant that mostly they starved until dinner. Dinner was a parsimonious serving of bread and butter. Saturdays, when they returned to Newark, were the best days. On those days, Elson could bathe, change, and obtain a hot meal.

After seven months in this work, George and Charlie were reunited. Like George, Charlie had been apprenticed as a sweep and learned all there was to know about cleaning chimneys. They decided to go into business for themselves. They left their employers with nothing but their clothes and had to buy the tools of their trade, down to the chimney hats, which they sewed themselves out of fabric, needle, and thread that they bought at the nearest village. They had to buy a scraper and a brush as well.

But there were plenty of chimneys that needed cleaning. They had no difficulty finding work, and their lots improved immediately. Finally, they were able to afford decent meals. In Nottingham, they briefly worked for another master, but they found the chimneys of that area even more difficult than the ones they had worked elsewhere. So they moved on. Elson remembers with great fondness the treatment he and his brother received from the monks of Charnwood Forest. These gentlemen led humble lives in a four-room cottage, augmented with a belfry and chapel. They were cultivating a garden in the many-acre forest that was their gift. It was the job of the Elson brothers to remove the soot from the monastery chimneys and deposit it in the garden as fertiliser. The monks fed them well – George remembered the soups in particular – and took a fatherly interest in the young men. They ended up spending several days with the monks, observing them in both their spiritual ceremonies and their gardening. Elson admired the enthusiasm that the monks brought to every endeavour.

The kindness of the monks was all it took for the brothers to remember their own family. Suddenly they longed to see their mother again, and they proceeded to Loughborough. The closer they got to home, the more trepidation they felt. They had, after all, run away with no warning. They were returning as fully employed tradesmen, but, as George notes, with understated bitterness, 'in such a trade'.[11] They hesitated so long at the edge of town that people they knew as children recognised them and told their mother where they were. Their stepfather, whom George generously refers to as just 'father', came to get them and bring them home. There, hot water, a change of clothes, and a loving, forgiving family awaited them.

Charlie and George acknowledged to themselves that they would dearly love to leave the chimney sweeping business. They had not chosen it; they had been 'gathered in its sooty embrace'.[12] But there was no other employment on offer. Still, they resolved to live, when possible, closer to their family, especially their mother. This meant looking for jobs closer to Loughborough. They were far too proud, however, to come home at the end of the day with no money. They would be broke and penniless again – often – but on those occasions they would keep apart from their mother, so as not to add to her financial burden. It bears remembering that, when they resolved this, George was 11 or 12 and Charlie was 14 or 15 years old.

The amount of sheer dirt they worked with, which chronically covered their clothes, hands, feet, and faces, kept them socially isolated. This much was illustrated when, one Sunday, they were idling by a river, and a stranger insisted they go to the nearby church. The boys pointed out the obvious: that they were covered in dirt and wouldn't be welcome, but the stranger showed up with some soap and kept insisting.

It was difficult for someone not in the chimney cleaning trade to understand just how adherent the dirt was. With water and soap, but no towels, the boys were barely able to smear the dirt around. They shocked everyone at the Ashby Folville church with their savage appearance. Then the pious villagers were shocked, again, when the brothers knew the liturgy and where, exactly, they were supposed to stand and sit. When the service was over, they fled.

However, when the same boys showed up at the evening service, the villagers remembered their better selves. A contingent of respectable children followed the Elsons back to the barn where they were sleeping, asked them questions, and in general, treated them as exotic, but harmless foreigners. They were gifted with food, and the next day, many people needed their chimneys cleaned. Even the vicarage had a chimney, and the vicar gave them socks and shoes.

Up until this time, the brothers had rather studiously avoided 'low company'. So it is difficult to know why they departed from this policy and joined up with some ruffians. It could have been the uncertainty of finding decent food and lodging from one day to the next. Or the social isolation may have crept up on them.

Whatever the reason, they briefly joined a band of sweeps and fertiliser salesmen who were cheating customers by misrepresenting the amount of fertiliser they were buying. Elson describes the ruse this way: 'tread the soot down hard in the strike-measure until it was half full and caked, then the loose soot added on top would be all that would run from the measure, effecting a saving of half a strike of soot each time.'[13] One savvy farmer caught them cheating him and called the constable. The men fled the scene, but they did not move far out of the vicinity. They were brazen thieves, often dodging tolls, and being so loud in taverns and public houses as to intimidate the surrounding company. They had been known to leave an inn in the morning without paying the bill.

The Elsons parted ways with these ruffians and found other, more respectable employers. These men were very poor, but shared what they had with their workers. They made their way back to the monastery where brand-new buildings had replaced the cottage. The new chimneys were much easier to navigate than old ones. By this time, Elson's skill as a climber had distinguished him. He was the one designated to climb all the chimneys at the abbey, which he did in a single day. Once again, the monks feasted the party with soup and roast beef.

George's younger brother trained as a sweep, and the Elson brothers moved in and out of one another's lives with regularity. For a time, George partnered with a 50-year-old married man named Tom Bale. A colourful personality, Bale was both a sweep and a celebrated fighter. In George's estimation, Bale could have been a champion but for his unfortunate habit of drinking to excess. Tom paid half a crown for a donkey, an important asset to a rural chimney sweep, because transporting soot and delivering it to farms that needed fertiliser was half the trade. Bale, Elson, and the donkey travelled the countryside, coring chimneys and hauling off cartloads of soot. The donkey did not bite, but had a wicked kick. To prevent this, Tom would hold one of the donkey's front legs, forcing it to deploy its other three legs in walking. Tom was literate, often reading the Bible and wanting to discuss its meaning, though he avoided church. He was a complex man who could reconcile Bible study with fighting and drinking to excess. At one point, he took George to a celebrated fight between two champions that was attended by 1,500 people.

In Braunston, Tom got drunk and agreed to a fight with a competitor in the chimney business. The fighters were reasonably well matched, but as the night wore on Tom's inebriation wore off, and he started winning. The fight was stopped by local law enforcement, but the fighters and their audience adjourned to another parish to resume it. According to George's testimony, Tom lost the fight when his opponent played dirty and broke his leg. In time, Tom got his revenge, beating his opponent badly enough that he needed several weeks to recover.

The social isolation of a sweep was such that George found himself mostly shunned by his family members. When he sought them out, aunts and uncles, even his grandmother, greeted him, fed him, and gave him money, but then these family members would find some excuse to not be in his company. George perhaps rightly attributed this to his chronic grime, and it caused him some bitter reflection.

He fell back on Tom's company. Because Tom was so well known for his fighting expertise, they were often feted at tap rooms. The two of them did not accept charity outright. But if a householder could not afford to get his chimney cleaned, he would often offer to give the sweeps some food. This kindness was never rejected.

In bad weather, Tom and George would seek shelter with the local blacksmith. Here was a trade, not quite as dirty as their own, but comparable. The smithies were always warm with metal-forging fires, and the smiths did not mind trading an afternoon of gossip. The smiths were generous hosts who would feed their sweeping guests, let them dry their clothes and warm their feet at the fire. In payment, George would sing them a song.

'I fancy now that I can hear the peculiar blowing of the huge bellows, the roar of the blazing fire, the clear, ringing sound of the hammer on the anvil, see the red sparks fly from off the red-hot iron,' wrote Elson many years later, when he had found an easier life. 'I sincerely wish long life and prosperity to the blacksmiths for all their kindness to the climbing boys of England.'[14]

Elson found that chimney work did not just involve removing soot, he was often called upon to do wildlife removal as well. Pigeons and other birds had to be scared out of the shafts where they had taken up residence. He once saved a cat. At one of the vicarages, he had to remove a bee colony. But what broke Elson's heart were the swallows' nests he had to remove. He admired the careful craftsmanship of the mud and clay structures, and the way the desperate parent birds would swoop and call at him, imploring him to desist. Whether the nest held eggs or tiny chicks, his heart went out, and he would not destroy the nestlings. Instead, he laid them carefully on top of some bricks, and then took the nest down to the householders to show them that the job was done.

George Elson's autobiography is nowhere stronger than the chapter he devotes to a working-class Christmas in Victorian England. Elson's employer, Tom Bale, determined that he would have a Christmas party, and he did not let his proximity to poverty get in the way of this dream. To put a bird on the table, he drove a goose into a dovecot, where the ungainly fowl struggled to free itself and became as blackened as a chimney sweep with the fresh soot that had just been applied to the dovecot by Bale. The farmer was summoned. At first, he too found the bird's predicament funny, but then he observed that the goose was lame. Bale convinced the farmer that the goose would not be marketable, and so he got his Christmas bird at a deep discount.

Bale next saw a three-legged table propped up against a wall. In return for fixing it, he cut a deal to use it for his dinner. A tinker sent around pots and pans wherewith to cook the holiday dishes. And other guests brought gifts of liquor. The dinner went well, as did the tea a few hours later. A gypsy (the term Elson used) regaled the assembled guests with a haunting melody that Elson heard for the first time. However, after tea, the heavy drinking started. Tom had managed to stay sober in order to keep his guests in line. When he saw their tempers starting to flare, he got them dancing. But the dance soon turned into fistfights and body slamming. The newly fixed table got smashed, and Tom threw his guests out of the house. Then he, his wife, and George sat down to the final Christmas meal of the day.

George had some regrets about leaving Tom Bale's employment, but there is no doubt that he upgraded to a better situation. Thanks to his brother, he found work among some wealthy gentry in Bedford. These people paid their sweeps well, treated them fairly, and, most importantly, were generous with meals. His employer at this time was a local preacher who carefully marshalled his financial resources, instead of spending them all on alcohol. So he was able to pay his sweeps a fair wage.

There was a gap in this preacher's generosity. He did not encourage his sweeps to attend church. Though Elson does not say so, the shocking presentation that chimney sweeps made in church was probably the reason. There was ever the problem of recalcitrant dirt. Also, they had no decent clothes. On Sundays, the preacher's sweeps stayed home where they improved their secular education with newspapers and any other reading matter they could afford, given their small wages. They got their hands on the *London Journal*, and read a serialised *Faust* that gave Elson a nightmare.

Elson had sustained injuries as a sweep, most notably a bad gash on the head. But none that left him permanently disabled. That was about to change. He was hired to clean an old chimney of a style he specifically disliked. In the process of cleaning, he lost his grip and fell many feet, tearing the skin off his foot down to the bone. The mistress of the house called a doctor and the foot was bandaged, but Elson had to walk eighteen miles back to his home base. Eventually, the foot healed, but it was badly scarred.

The story of an angry gamekeeper illustrates just how few protections Victorian working children had. On their way to a job, Elson and his fellow sweep saw some birds and they threw a stick and brush at them for the joy of seeing them fly up in the air. Their gamekeeper chased them, and they ran. But later in the day, it turned out that the keeper had been tracking them. He enlisted some other townsfolk to stop the boys and hold them, while he gave Elson a severe beating. While the laws of private game preserves did allow for the punishment of poachers, the boys had not poached. They had not even injured the game birds. Elson felt that the gamekeeper should face justice, but no grown-up who heard the story felt it his duty to bring the keeper up on charges. It took months for Elson to fully heal from injuries inflicted by the gamekeeper; meanwhile, he did his physically demanding work in pain and found sleeping difficult.

Elson accidentally gave notice to his employers. He asked to go bathe in the river and, somehow, was taken for resigning his place. He found himself with 13 shillings, looking once more for work, but alone, not accompanied by one of his brothers or a friend. In this solitary state, he found himself briefly engaged to a criminal master sweep, much like Dickens's Gamfield. He agreed to work for this man and spent the night in a room with two small children, Nick and Tony, who were also in the master's employ. Tony was an orphan and Nick came from an abusive home and alcoholic parents from whom he had run away. The master sweep rousted these boys from bed at three in the morning and sent them to clean a chimney that was a two-hour walk away. They had no shoes and had to walk over ground that was not just stony, but covered with frost. While cleaning the chimney, Tony dropped a grate on his foot and cried out. The mistress of the house ministered to his injury. Then she saw that his feet were covered with sores not related to the most recent mishap. Then and there, she decided to separate Tony from his employer and she sent word, through Nick, that Tony would not be returning to his lodgings or his job.

This was the story, as George heard it, when Nick returned. That was enough for George. He left his new master and tried to get Nick to go with him. But Nick was too frightened. Though he was far from wealthy, George did have a small fortune relative to what sweeps usually possessed. He still had a few shillings from his last job, his own brush and chimney cap, and a semi-decent suit of clothes, including a swallowtail coat which was far too large for him, but presentable. With these accoutrements, he set out to find his family.

His mother and stepfather were taking advantage of the beautiful weather to conduct brisk sales in earthenware. By now, George was big enough to carry a basket full of merchandise on his head, so he spent the season with his parents, hawking pots and camping out. George's mother demonstrated her talent for outdoor cooking, and they had some lovely picnics. They drank spring water, then fell asleep under their wagon, having put a blanket around the wheels to form a skirt of sorts. In this way, the family spent a beautiful summer.

The pot hawkers had permission under English law to camp out on the side of the roads. It was an unfairly applied law; England's gypsies did not have the same rights. However, the gypsies were enterprising. Seeing the Elson family, with their pots, camped out, a few dozen of these travellers set up camp right next to them, using the Elsons as cover. The potters were astonished at how quickly the gypsies set up their tents. An officer of the law came by and yelled 'Are you potsmen?' to which all the gypsies yelled in reply that they were. The potters and gypsies slept in tents side by side with no incident and all decamped quickly in the morning.[15]

Cold weather and shorter days soon put an end to this gorgeous idyll. George and his brother returned to chimney sweeping. George's upward mobility did not proceed in anything like a straight line. After twelve months of sweeping, during which the Elsons were able to bank some savings, they bought a horse, cart, and harness. This was an important upgrade to any chimney sweeping business. Chimney soot could be retained for use as fertiliser, and it was desirable to transport this fertiliser from chimney to farm or garden. However, it seems they overpaid for their transportation. The horse was mostly blind, and after a few months, and a few breakdowns, they sold the whole array – horse, cart, harness – at a steep loss.

In Chatteris, George encountered a new challenge: 'treacle chimneys'. Because the locals were burning turf, the soot of their chimneys was a slippery, woolly mixture. This required some dexterity. George found that he had to climb quickly before the wet soot carried him down the chimney with it. Nevertheless, he managed to master these chimneys as well.

After surviving a bout of rheumatic fever, which nearly killed him, George contracted himself for a year to a well-off master in Sleaford. There, he had the good fortune of sweeping for several great houses. He was impressed with the décor, but what was most meaningful to him was the delicious food he was served. When the table was laid for the servants, the sweeps were invited to join in. They had venison, beef, coffee, and ale – for breakfast. Such nourishment must have seemed like rare jewels to George Elson, who was frequently hungry and never seemed to have enough warm clothes.

It was a convention of chimney sweeping that the client hosted meals. In all George's negotiations with various masters, no alternate provision for meals was ever made. The master sweep, like the other sweeps, sat down to eat at the expense of his clients or went hungry if no meal was offered. At some houses, they were presented with bread, cheese, and a tankard of very strong ale which, though it was mouldy, the sweeps demolished, even if they had to steel themselves to finish it. Who knew when those kinds of calories would come around again? George noted that the ale made him feel like a king, but the reader can also see in his telling of this story, the ambivalence toward drink that would eventually cause him to embrace total sobriety.

George contracted to work for his Sleaford employer for two years, but found that this master had trouble paying him. George's initial impression of the man was that he was respectable and ran an efficient business. Weeks passed, and George got to watch, first-hand, as his employer sank into alcoholism. This master sweep spent more and more time in public houses and then posed a danger to himself and George when he drove his horse and cart under the influence. George, young as he still was, had the presence of mind to demand that he himself drive the cart when his master was too drunk to drive safely.

The irresponsible behaviour of his employer put George in a difficult situation. Technically, he had sealed himself to this master for two years. But the missing wages and alcoholism drove him to break that contract. George left Sleaford with his brother, having first secured his possessions away from his employer's house to protect those items from misappropriation. By this time, the Elson brothers had put together a surprisingly good collection of books. Despite his dirty clothes and poverty, George found that many people enjoyed and even sought out his company. His beautiful singing voice and his repertoire of memorised songs helped make him popular, as did his book knowledge. Therefore, George and his brother embarked on a walking and reading tour of north England.

Though he usually enjoyed his treks across the English countryside, George suffered a quantum of harassment, too. People often assumed that sweeps were disreputable. In Hull, the Elson brothers were arrested and had to go to the police station where they were interrogated, though nothing was charged against them. Children would yell at him, tamper with his gear, etc. He astutely observed that it was the job of the grown-ups attached to these children to bring them in line, but they did not. Worse, they would use the blackened appearance of the chimney sweep as a bogeyman, telling their children, when George appeared, 'Here's the bogey come to put you in his black bag.'[16] At a store, when a coin rolled under the furniture, the shopkeeper accused him of stealing it. George turned out his pockets, to show they were empty of the coin, but the shopkeeper then accused him of swallowing the coin and sent round for the police. Eventually, the coin was recovered by someone using a cane. George felt that the twopence and halfpenny he was offered for the time he spent under suspicion was insulting.

When he was around 20 years old, George made his way to London. His autobiography does not say when he learned to use the chimney sweeping 'machine', or where he obtained such a device, but in London, he owned and was skilled with one of these machines. One assumes he was referring to the invention of Joseph Glass, who devised a non-motorised device with extendable rods and brass screw joints added to a solid cane stem. This machine was invented in 1828, and it eliminated the need for children to climb chimneys, but, as with many advancements, it was slow to be adopted.

This machine, however, made it possible for George to remain in a profession which he might otherwise have outgrown. He continued climbing as needed, where the chimneys were wide enough, but the device could be used in dangerously narrow flues and where the chimney turned a corner or was craggy. As a grown man operating a sophisticated device in London, he finally earned decent wages. The bustle of London contrasted sharply with the country life George had previously led. He found that most of his colleagues spent their earnings on alcohol, and he joined them often. But he perceived the danger in doing so, and moved to a quiet lodging in the West End.

As a young man, George chafed at how little he had achieved in life. He felt, again, that his education was neglected and that his trade limited his advancement in life. He made a point of improving his reading agenda, and set himself the task of reading *The History of England* by Hume and Smollett in its entirety. He also read Shakespeare, Cowper, and Burns. He kept up with current events by reading the *News of the World* daily. He learned how to follow the doings of Parliament and the debates in the House of Commons. He went to the theatre when he could. By the time he was in his early 20s, he had seen *Macbeth* and *Hamlet*.

Part of George's transformation into a Londoner was the adoption of congregationalism. He became a member of a Congregationalist chapel and also a member of the Young Men's Christian Association, serving as a committee member for eleven years. He attended church twice on Sundays and often visited the dissenting churches as well as the Church of England in order to get various perspectives on faith. Though Elson does not say so in his book, his pursuit of comparative theologies was an important part of his intellectual development.

In his quest for self-improvement, George became a teetotaller for life. It was not a whim. He researched the issue, read the science on it, and became a moderate drinker for a year prior to taking the temperance pledge. George had seen first-hand how damaging addiction to alcohol could be. His own father's untimely death had been related to inebriation. And, in dying, George's father had dragged his family down from their foothold in the middle class. His friend and nominal employer Tom Bale, a man of great skill, also failed to fulfil his potential because he was too fond of a pint. His more recent employer, a man who, at least initially, gave the impression of organisation and respectability, had fallen into the perils of drink, right before George's eyes. We also know that George keenly valued his mind; it made sense to protect that treasure.

However, one incident in particular seems to have scared George into sobriety. He met his brother at a public house and some guardsmen encouraged them to drink to excess. Upon leaving the establishment, both brothers struggled with their balance. Some locked gates blocked the way to his home, so George climbed the Hyde Park fence because the park provided a shortcut to his lodging. A policeman saw him and gave chase. In the process, George tore a trouser leg and somehow made it home. He came to no real harm. But it shocked him that, in the morning, he had no recollection of escaping the police. He could not remember running through the park, crossing the bridge over the Serpentine, or even climbing into bed.

George does not tell his readers which temperance organisation he was aligned with. It may have been the British Temperance League. That organisation's pledge committed the signer to 'abstain from all liquors of an intoxicating quality … except as medicines'. Like Alcoholics Anonymous, the temperance movement in Victorian England provided an alternative social network for people who wished to stay sober. George stayed active with this group and cherished his sobriety pledge card, dated 27 January 1857. As an active member of the temperance movement, George became involved in defeating the Wine Licences Bill, and he attended a session of the House of Commons for that purpose.

George Elson was an intellectually curious man, and highly intelligent, as evidenced by the wit and rhetorical flourishes that often decorate his autobiography. He was almost entirely self-taught.

His reader may think it a pity that such a man did not have more formal education and more opportunities. His story shows us, among other things, how irreversible a slide into poverty was for the average Victorian family.

In London, however, George discovered where the educational opportunities for a working man had been hidden: in private 'societies'. These clubs generally charged only a shilling or two a year in dues, and they had libraries. Books were expensive, but these libraries offered a nearly unlimited opportunity to read collections that had been curated by contemporary thinkers. These clubs also offered lectures and discussions. Elson became a sharp political animal by listening to and participating in these debates.

The greater opportunities afforded by London and his improved self-care combined to give George the success he had yearned for. He went into business for himself and got married. The birth of two children followed. He ascended to the top of his field. He became his mother's main source of financial support until her death in 1863.

In 1866, George was about to clean the chimney of a well-to-do house when the servants observed an open window and signs of a break-in. They spotted the burglars in the garden, and George chased them, calling for help. They were large men, and there were three of them; no one wanted to help George, but he followed them through several streets. Finally, they confronted George and beat him. One of them deployed a lethal bludgeon which George called a 'life preserver'. They held George down and beat him with this weapon. George believed they intended to murder him. Somehow, he got back on his feet, calling for help. The timely appearance of a man with a rifle at a nearby window saved George. The criminals fled the scene, George badly wounded, but still following. Finally, four stone masons appeared. They chased the burglars and captured them, whereupon, with their help, George took the criminals to the police station.

George bore witness against the men who assaulted him. They had many previous offences and stood trial at the Old Bailey. Only during Elson's narration of the trial does the reader learn that George is quite a small man. When all eyes were on him, the hero of the story, someone in the audience audibly muttered, 'What, that little fellow?'[17] The men were sentenced to hard labour. The youngest got ten years, another got fifteen years, and the one who had attacked George with the preserver got twenty years.

George's injuries were terrible, and he was unable to work for some time. News of his heroic deeds and injuries travelled, however, and many people donated money for his care and the sustenance of his family. Altogether, £60 were raised. Elson received another £10 from the court out of consideration for his testimony and the injuries he received bringing the men to justice.

Medical treatment failed to alleviate George's pain. What finally made him feel better were cold baths. As a consequence, he developed the lifetime habit of swimming, initially in the Serpentine River, then in many different bodies of water. He even travelled to Margate to swim in the ocean. As a daily swimmer, he would wash off most of the toxic carcinogens in which he worked. Chimney sweeps were at risk of cancer, especially if they did not die as children. Perhaps in alleviating his pain, George stumbled on a health measure that prolonged his life. Daily swimming also had the virtue of rendering George fresh and clean looking when he presented himself in social situations. This would prove to be invaluable to his self-esteem.

Still aching from the injuries he had suffered in apprehending the house breakers, George attended a protest on behalf of Gladstone's 1866 reform bill. In an attempt to stifle the protest, the police had occupied Hyde Park and closed the gates. Reformers stormed the gates, bringing them down, and a bloody conflict ensued between the protesters and the police. Injured parties on both sides were taken to nearby St George's hospital. Footmen arrived and brandished their bayonets.

The next protest went far more smoothly. Hyde Park peacefully fulfilled its destiny as a venue for free expression of political thought. Universal suffrage for men was hotly defended by various speakers. Elson's memoir almost never discusses politics, but he defends the

Hyde Park protests, noting that the practice of one man, one vote was only fair, and that it was also inevitable and would come about no matter who was in power: 'Reform agitation for the franchise … was a good and lawful cause, and was bound to become law sooner or later by either a Conservative or Liberal Government.'[18]

Elson sold his London business and moved his family to Teddington, Middlesex where he became a member of the Mutual Instruction Society. Such societies existed in towns and cities all over England where they fostered learning, debate, and musical performances. They were also the handmaidens of sobriety, offering the same lively social interchange that pubs offered, but without the pressure to stand a round. George was enormously honoured to be appointed secretary to this organisation, a position that came with a sinecure of £5 a year, equal in value to approximately £742 today. For a young man whose salary had been £2 annually, just a few years earlier, it was a triumph. 'There was I, a full-fledged secretary of a substantial institution … who for long years had been, as it were, an outcast of society as a climbing boy … and now, while yet a chimney-sweep, thought worthy of a post of trust and reward like the one in question.'[19] Elson did credit to this position, increasing membership and collecting dues from reluctant members.

Elson himself led a discussion on the topic of chivalry, in which he argued (not for the first time over the centuries) that, yes, it is dead. Other speakers hastened to chivalry's defence, providing, it is assumed, contemporary examples of its living, breathing practice. He considered that he lost the debate, but was gracious in defeat.

As a result of his sobriety and participation in intellectual and political societies, George met people who felt strongly that he had not achieved his potential, and they told him so. 'People often told me I ought not to follow such a business, that, with my personal appearance and rising ability, I should try to obtain something better … It is astonishing how dissatisfied a person becomes with his position when he is assured it is beneath him.'[20]

George was receptive to this message; it resonated strongly with what he felt about himself, that chimney sweeping was a livelihood into which he had been hoodwinked. Such a trade may have been inevitable when his family was plunged into poverty, but now he had educated friends, a mind improved by reading, and oratorical skills.

At this point, George would have been around 40, the age at which some would argue that a man achieves his peak. Because he had started work as a very young child, he had now been sweeping for thirty years. Looking back, George estimates he swept hundreds of thousands of chimneys, sometimes thirty before breakfast, often fifty in a single day.

It was not only a low-status line of work; it was empirically dangerous. And to be hurt or disabled, it wasn't even necessary to fall down the chimney shaft; one could easily fall off a roof. Climbing down, he had learned, was the tricky part. Going up, the climber could see where to grab hold, but 'on coming down, the feet have to feel the way over sharp and dangerous points, the most likely place to slip, and one slight mistake is enough to ensure a terrible fall.'[21]

Lately, as he reached the safety of the chimney's floor, his knees and legs trembled. He became aware just how lucky he had been. So many children died or became disabled as a result of chimney climbing. 'Although I actually escaped to tell the tale, it was more than hundreds of other poor climbing boys were able to do – they having fallen victims to its exposures, privations, and many dangers.'[22]

George sold his sweeping business and used the capital to open a shop in Hereford where he sold maps and charts. He became, like his father, a travelling salesman, but with a different sort of merchandise, one which called on his talent and intellect. He sold maps to businessmen and teachers, canvassing a wide region, often walking thirty miles in a day. Out amongst the farms of Herefordshire, he found himself embroiled in the conflict between farmers and their poorly paid workers who were then agitating for better pay. The workers, Elson observes, were 'dwarfed' and skinny, living in hovels. Elson deplored the tradition of paying the workers part of their wages in cider.

George's readers will find it amusing that the farmers suspected him of being an agent for reform, and the farm workers assumed he belonged to the privileged classes. Elson, a Gladstonian reformer, assured the workers that his sympathies lay with them. When talking to the farmers, he asked if they would like to buy a map.

It is not entirely clear why Elson abandoned the sale of maps. But there was another skill he had been quietly developing for the past several years: swimming. One day, when he was out for his usual swim, he had saved a child from drowning, and this incident may have made him bold enough to consider how he could turn his love of the water into a career. When he read an advertisement in a newspaper for a swimming instructor, he saw his chance.

The business turned out to be a Turkish bathhouse with a swimming pool. The owner needed a swimming instructor who could also do 'shampoos'. In the world of Turkish bathing, 'shampoos' referred, confusingly enough, to massage. George agreed to learn the latter skill, and he was hired. He moved with his family to Leamington to pursue an entirely new line of work. In time, his wife would learn the art of shampoo and join him in this profession. Bathing was mostly segregated by sex, and women preferred to be ministered to by other women. With a second income, the Elson family fortunes rose quickly. That was a good thing because George and his wife had six children altogether.

Turkish baths had become all the rage in Victorian England. The bathing experience typically involved sitting in a sauna, which featured drier air than its cultural precedents. Then a massage might follow, and the event would be finished off with a plunge into cold water or a shower, possibly administered by the masseur.

While doctors often told patients to avoid the baths, many people believed that 'bathing' had enormous health benefits. The truth was, of course, somewhere in the middle. Heat, especially humid heat, could improve circulation and alleviate the symptoms of arthritis and other joint degeneration. It could be quite therapeutic to people with chronic pain. Perhaps most importantly, it was fun and could lower stress which is the root cause of a myriad of health problems.

The heat of the sauna-like bathhouse took some adjusting to, but George learned to tolerate it. His students came, as many as fifty at a time, from as far away as Malvern. He was also called upon to give swimming lessons to blind students.

Elson came to believe strongly in the medical benefits of his work. And he had good enough reasons to think that many doctors were wrongfully withholding the health benefits of bathing from their patients. Observing that there was no easily accessible information that summarised these benefits, he wrote a pamphlet about the benefits of bathing which he had printed in the thousands. The pamphlet received a favourable review in the local newspaper, and George sent copies to all the bathhouses in England. The proprietors of those businesses bought the pamphlets in bulk directly from Elson, one bathhouse ordered a thousand at one time. Over time, he was able to sell all his pamphlets and even turned a small profit.

Work that one believes in is always more enjoyable, and George's days were filled with a strong sense of purpose, only somewhat marred by the occasional grumpy customer. Leamington also featured a good library, in which George continued his lifelong self-education. He also took up fox hunting, on foot, and often ran forty miles in a day. He came to know the forests well, and frequently chased the fox more successfully than those on horseback. No one could fox hunt on foot better than he, George surmised. This was a physically demanding hobby, but George maintained excellent health through his 40s and 50s, as least partly as a result. He was proud to write that he did not miss a day of work for fourteen years.

As a 'shampooer', George was already engaged in the work of massage, but he decided to qualify as a 'masseur', one who was, presumably, better acquainted with the workings of the muscles and the medical uses of massage. He had his house remodelled to accommodate facilities for massage and 'hydrotherapy', a term for water treatment, which often involves exercising in warm water, though Elson did not write about the specifics of his treatment.

He found fewer customers than he wished. The Turkish bathhouse for which he had previously worked identified his new practice, perhaps with some justice, as competition. George felt that, having done the additional study needed to call himself a masseur and hydrotherapist, his services were different from and superior to those offered at the bathhouse. Nevertheless, his former employer was jealous of Elson's customers and made them feel uncomfortable about patronising both businesses.

One of his Leamington customers encouraged him to move north and promised that he would recommend him to friends and associates. Four of George's children had, by this time, left home, so he moved his household yet again. Elson never identifies the northern English town in which he lived by name, but here, finally, he achieved the status and recognition he had been pursuing all his life. He and his wife, who continued working alongside him, were able to live in a big house and keep a servant. What was more meaningful to George, however, was the respect with which he was treated, especially by customers. Some of them would send a carriage for him. He entered by the front door, not through the kitchen, the servants were respectful. They took his coat and silk hat. He sometimes ate a meal with the family, not the servants.

This was his heyday. But competitors emerged and cut into his business. He moved again, this time to the south of England where he began his autobiography. His wife had asked him not to publish his memoirs while they lived in the north, for fear it would hurt their status. He deferred to her wishes, but also noted that there was no shame in having started life as a climbing boy. Elson was born in 1833. When he published his autobiography, in 1900, he was 67. As Elson notes, his story is the only first-person account of a Victorian chimney sweep, published in book form and non-fiction. But it is also important in challenging the notion of class immobility in Victorian England. Elson not only survived in a dangerous profession, he rose, changed professions more than once, achieved financial success, and social eminence. His life story absolutely defies the pervading assumption that Victorians were stuck in whatever condition they were born. *The Last of the Climbing Boys* is much more of a Horatio Alger story than the typical Victorian novel, in which the characters ascend only by marriage or inheritance, if they are lucky and do not 'fall'. As such, it has much in common with the rags-to-riches tales of the twentieth century.

One might argue that Elson was exceptional and therefore not a typical Victorian. But there is much more in his story about hard work and making good choices than about being exceptional. As a boy, he chose to be a lifelong worker, and he invested his energy in socialising with intellectuals rather than squandering it on booze and watching fights and Punch and Judy shows. A good marriage and lifelong habits of exercise and hygiene no doubt helped him rise to a better condition than what he left home in. These are habits that anyone could cultivate – which seems to be the point of his book.

Chapter 7

Twists Triumphant:
How Matchstick Girls Demanded More

Not all poor children in London were orphans. Many families travelled to the brink of poverty and fell right over its edge into the abyss just from having more children than the parents' combined incomes would support. It behoves us to remember that, but for a timely inheritance from an observant relative, Charles Dickens's own family might have lived a life much like Martha Robertson's.

In 1882, Martha was born to George and Jane Robertson. Both parents had been born in Bethnal Green and never escaped. By the year 1900, Bethnal Green's unrepaired houses and overcrowding would make it one of London's worst slums. Here, and in neighbouring Whitechapel, Jack the Ripper carried out his murders with impunity. George and Jane lived in two rooms on Harold Street with their nine children. That would have been palatial, by working-class standards of the day, except that they also shared those same two rooms with two more families, bringing the grand total of that small residence to twenty-one. The blight and poverty of Harold Street have subsequently been wiped off the map, but while it existed, Harold Street made it into Charles Booth's notes as an area of 'chronic want'.[1]

Martha began doing freelance work for the Bryant & May matchstick factory when she was 6 years old, or possibly younger. Her mother, Jane Robertson, was employed at the same company and introduced Martha to the work. Jane raised a family of nine children, so she desperately needed work she could do at home, and Bryant & May allowed freelance contractors to do various tasks, especially box assembly, from home. From a very young age, Martha helped Jane make her quota, whether at home or in the factory. It was Martha, exclusively, who delivered the assembled boxes to the factory.[2]

As did many working children, Martha began her day at 5.00 am. Her immediate chores were household. It was her job to clean out the remains of yesterday's fire and start a new fire. She dressed herself as best she could, using a pile of communal shoes in the cupboard under the stairs. She did not always find a matching pair, but no matter. Whether in shoes that matched or otherwise, she walked to the Bryant & May match and matchbox factory and got in the queue with other children and adults who found work there.[3]

Martha's arrangement with Bryant & May was typical. It was piece work. She was paid for exactly the amount of work she did, and this was very carefully measured. For 2 ½ d, she made one 'gross' of matchboxes. With a small sum in hand, she then returned home, first buying a breakfast of bread and milk for her family.

Her mother Jane had brought Martha into the Bryant & May sphere. Jane seems to have worked more or less full-time as a box maker for that company. There was a great deal of fluidity for freelancers. Jane and Martha seem to have worked some shifts at the factory and, at other times, filled up the floors of their small residence and worked from home. This at-home work was no small feat because the boxes had to be spread out in order to dry, and they were easy to break while curing, making it difficult for the twenty-one people who lived in those two rooms to use the space. By necessity, small children had to leave the house and amuse themselves on the street until they were old enough to start working.

Under British law of that time, Martha was mandated to attend school, at least part-time, from the ages of 5 to 10. This compulsory education aimed less at teaching fundamental skills, like reading, writing, and maths, than it did at making very poor working families content with their lot in life and unlikely to revolt. Religion was the primary instrument for pacifying the potential malcontents who might, at any moment, realise that they worked fourteen hours a day to starve, and take to the streets with firebrands. The middle and upper classes lived in uneasy fear of such a rebellion. They had a general sense that the lives of the poor were unbearable and that businesses made money by literally starving their workers, workers who routinely included children under 14. Predictably, guilt was converted to fear and fear into blaming the victim.

Under the educational system of that day, girls were even more poorly taught than boys. While boys might have a shot at learning something of academic value, girls learned things like punctuality, prudery, tidiness, minding the baby, and, interestingly, fire starting, which Martha would have already learned from her mother, with or without formal schooling. Victorian journalist George Sims, well known as a bon vivant himself, praised the late Victorian girls' curriculum for teaching girls a sense of shame as well as suppressing any tendency to flirt.[4] Science had finally been introduced into the common curriculum in the 1880s, but Martha was ineligible to study science; those classes were reserved for boys.

Boys were under a great deal more pressure to attend school than girls were. A document from 1890 specifies that boys are not to miss classes to take care of their siblings unless there is no sister at home to do that work. As a late middle child in her family, with three younger siblings, Martha would often have had a baby or toddler in her arms. Babysitting would have taken precedence over attending school. Martha might have escorted her younger siblings to school at the expense of her own learning opportunities.

Regardless of what she may or may not have learned at school, Martha's education was over at the age of 13. That is when she started working full-time at Bryant & May. If current research has her birth date correct, this would have been in 1895, seven years after the famous matchgirl strike which forced the public to note the conditions at the Bryant & May factory. However, Martha worked, as a piece worker, for Bryant & May as an even younger child, and was likely aware of the strike. She may even have been one of the child workers who left the assembly lines and strode out on the street the day of the strike.

Who were Bryant & May?

William Bryant and Francis May were Quakers. As such, the greed that characterised other ruthless capitalists of the early industrial era might seem unexpected in them. To put the Bryant & May enterprise entirely into context, it must be noted that Quakers, like Unitarians and other non-Anglicans, came in for a share of discrimination that very palpably hurt their financial prosperity. Quakers were barred from pursuing careers in law, medicine, the Church of England, and the military. That left business, and in the late nineteenth century, business had moved away from dispersed cottage industries helmed by skilled craftsmen. Automation and mass production were in the driver's seat. Many enterprising Quakers, therefore, became industrialists.

If we go back far enough in time, we learn that matches were actually invented to make fire starting safer. Lighting a fire with a cloth or a piece of paper is always a risky business, and could pretty easily lead to the loss of a home or business due to a runaway fire. When Bryant and May first started their partnership, they were importing safety matches from Sweden. However, demand for matches in England grew quickly. People did not want to lose their homes in the effort to start dinner. Soon Sweden could not export enough matches. May obtained a patent on a newly designed match in 1861, and the partners leased factory space in Bow. That became the Fairfields Works. By 1876, Bryant & May had employed approximately 5,000 workers, and they had become prominent employers in London's east end.

In her admirable history of the 1888 strike, Louise Raw writes that Francis May was a kind man, a true Quaker. Similar testimony finds William Bryant a more 'forceful' man.[5] Nevertheless, early reports on the conditions at the factory suggest it was not yet the hell hole it would become. In those early days, the Children's Employment Commission investigated the factory, found it spacious, and even interviewed a sampling of the child labourers. Some of these children had worked at other matchstick factories and had good things to say about this one. Tellingly, some children thought they were better treated and better paid at Fairfields Works than at other industries.

Over the years, conditions declined. The death of William Bryant was the decisive change. Bryant had brought his four sons into the business. Over time, the five Bryants marginalised May. Wilberforce Bryant took the reins after his father William's death in 1874. Where William and May had run their business in some conformance with Quaker ideals, the Bryant boys did not feel so shackled. Wilberforce and his brother, Frederick Bryant, may have converted to the Church of England. Doing so would have admitted the brothers to the full privileges afforded to Anglican businessmen – including protection from prosecution vis-à-vis employee abuses.

The Bryants bought up two other companies, then restructured the enterprise as a limited liability corporation. Wilberforce adopted the title of chairman, while his brother Frederick became managing director. They upgraded their machinery, bought advertising, and schmoozed newspaper reporters and editors. Then the company proceeded to gobble up other, smaller matchmaking companies. In 1876, just two years after the death of the progenitor William, the Bryant company was the main employer of matchmakers. By 1885, they were exporting their products to the United States, Asia, and Australia. This allowed them to lower all wages and pocket more profits. When the reformer Annie Besant became interested in Bryant & May, in the late 1880s, they were paying wages lower than they had paid twelve years previously. Besant rightly called the Bryants out for running a monopoly, and she pointed to one woman with fifteen years' experience who had been making 20 shillings a week. At the point of Besant's investigations, that same employee was now making little more than 5 shillings a week.

The Bryants were able to exploit a loophole in labour law known as the sweating system which originated in the clothing industry. As you might guess, the sweating system was the forerunner of the sweat shop. 'Sweaters', as these unfortunate employees were called, were officially sub-contractors or piece workers. They performed a specific number of tasks for a specific fixed price. In the Bryant & May factory, frame fillers received a shilling for 100 completed frames, cutters earned less than 3 shillings for three gross of boxes, and packers got 1 shilling and ninepence per 100 boxes they wrapped up.

Annie Besant's 'White Slavery' Report

This book has examined many ways in which the Victorian era failed children, especially children of the poor. So perhaps it is time to acknowledge that the Victorian era also featured many beautiful folkways. Not the least of these was that a reformer could overtly identify as socialist without being marginalised by the political infrastructure.

Such a socialist and reformer was Annie Besant. The child exploitation at Bryant & May first came under Besant's scrutiny when she learned what dividends the company was paying its shareholders, and then contrasted that with what they were paying their workers. The company was consistently paying well over 20 per cent returns on investment, and that return had risen to 38 per cent at one point. Besant made absolutely no bones about claiming that these high returns were derived from the starvation wages paid to employees. The highest paid workers made 13 shillings a week, and only four women employees made this amount. In an article titled 'White Slavery in London', Besant noted the piece work payment system and the long hours. Employees started work at 6.30 am, except in the winter months when the workday started at 8.00 am. They stood on their feet the entire day. One half hour was allotted for breakfast, and the same for dinner. It was customary for factory workers to eat breakfast after working an hour or more of their shifts.[6]

To illustrate just how little their wages covered, Besant invoked the example of a 16-year-old girl and her sister who both worked at Bryant & May. They lived in one room. Their diet consisted entirely of bread, butter, and tea, except for rare occasions when marmalade and coffee were added to this abstemious meal. Besant's spirited 16-year-old subject attended a show at the Paragon on occasion, when someone else paid for her ticket, 'and that appeared to be the solitary bit of colour in her life',[7] Besant notes.

The low wages and inhuman tax on the human skeleton were not the whole story at Bryant & May, though. Poorly paid workers also paid fines for trivial offences, such as leaving a few matches on a bench. The fine for that could be as much as threepence, and threepence could also be deducted from wages for talking, leaving a bench untidy, or even having dirty feet. Several historians have noted the cruelty of fining dirty feet on employees who are not paid enough to buy shoes. If an employee was late to work, she was locked out for half her shift, and also fined a penny.

The higher fine of 1 shilling was generally reserved for inadvertently striking a match. Such an accident was more or less inevitable during the quick handling of matches. Speed was of the essence in making the most money possible from piece work. If a struck match damaged a frame, the worker could be sacked.

One girl was fined a shilling for letting some webbing get caught up in the machinery. She had allowed that to happen in the process of saving her fingers from being cut off. Her supervisor told her, 'never mind about your fingers'. But it did pay to save one's fingers, as another employee would learn when she lost one and received no financial support from the company. Perhaps the final straw on these conditions was a foreman who felt free to hit his female employees. One employee Besant interviewed indicated that he hit workers randomly 'when he is mad'.[8]

Besant argued that Bryant & May could never have achieved such high returns if they had used chattel slaves, because the expense of feeding, clothing, and housing official slaves would cost more than what the company was currently paying most of its employees. Also, slaves have value in their person, and the easy dismissal and starvation of Bryant & May employees showed that they had no personal value to their employer. 'Born in slums, driven to work while still children, undersized because underfed, oppressed because helpless, flung aside as soon as worked out, who cares if they die or go on the streets, provided only that the Bryant and May shareholders get their 23 per cent,' Besant wrote, adding, 'Oh if we had but a people's Dante, to make a special circle in the Inferno for those who live on this misery, and suck wealth out of the starvation of helpless girls.'[9]

Phossy Jaw

Besant had a blind spot in her compassion for the matchstick girls. In citing the many atrocities committed at Bryant & May, she overlooked the problem of phossy jaw. The scientific term is phosphorus necrosis of the jaw, and it is what it sounds like: deterioration of the jawbone.

A photo of some of the Bryant & May strikers clearly shows us what phossy jaw looked like. In this photo, two women, front and centre, have distorted mouths. Their lower lips are distended and look as if they were being pulled to one side. In both women, a fistula to the side of the mouth advertises that they are victims of the middle stages of jaw necrosis.

Phossy jaw was specific to workers in matchstick factories in the nineteenth and early twentieth centuries. The condition has been eradicated by better factory conditions and changes to match production. In its early stages, phossy jaw caused swollen and painful gums and toothaches. As it progressed, teeth would fall out, and oozing, foul-smelling abscesses would form. The bone of the jaw would start to die, and the dead tissue would separate from the still living tissue. The jawbone would continue to deteriorate, causing massive facial disfigurement. Victims of phossy jaw found that they glowed in the dark, with chins that radiated a weird greenish white glow. In some cases, phossy jaw caused brain damage which led to seizures. The condition was fatal if left untreated. Infections caused by the abscesses eventually led to multiple organ failure. The patient could be saved by surgery in which the dead jaw material was removed. However, if the disease had progressed to a point of ruining most of the jaw, the patient could be left with nutritional deficits, related to difficulty eating. Where the patient had access to antibiotics, they could be used to stop the disease from progressing.

This syndrome was caused by exposure to the white phosphorus in matches. Match factory workers absorbed the chemical through the air. Phossy jaw was discovered and immediately linked to the matchmaking industry by the Viennese physician Friedrich Wilhelm Lorinser almost fifty years prior to the matchgirl strike at Bryant & May. By 1844, Lorinser had published his results and established the cause of the disease beyond any reasonable doubt by documenting twenty-two cases. That same year, Swedish inventor Gustaf Erik Pasch patented the use of red phosphorus. Matches produced with red phosphorus were much safer, not just for factory workers, but also for consumers. Among the other virtues of these new matches was their lower chance of igniting spontaneously in high temperatures. By 1872, Finland, then a duchy of Russia, had outlawed the use of white phosphorus in match production. Denmark followed suit two years later. The technology to save their workers from jaw necrosis was available to the Bryants and May a solid forty-four years before their mostly female and largely childlike labour force finally walked out on the job.

Strike and March

While exposing conditions at Bryant & May, Besant told an interesting story of an early employee action that foreshadowed the strike and march of 5 and 6 July 1888. When he was alive and active in the factory management, Theodore Bryant commissioned a statue of Prime Minister William Gladstone. Gladstone is popularly remembered as a liberal who championed the working man. To pay for this memorial, T. Bryant forced his own workers to pay a shilling each out of their pay. Then he closed the factory for half a day, calling it a worker 'holiday', unpaid, of course. Clearly, this was out of tune with what shoeless factory workers actually wanted – which was their full wages and the most billable hours possible. When you only make 4 shillings a week, you need all the shillings and all the hours. 'We don't want no holidays,' one girl told Besant.[10]

When the statue was unveiled, many of these impoverished girls went to the ceremony with stones and even bricks in their pockets. 'I was conscious of a wish that some of those bricks had made an impression on Mr Bryant's conscience,' Besant wrote. Afterwards, some of the girls surrounded the statue and cut themselves, drizzling Gladstone's marble effigy with their blood as if to say it had been built with their blood.[11]

Besant is sometimes inaccurately credited with organising the famous matchgirls' strike and march of 5 and 6 July 1888. But Besant's relationship with the match workers was more complex and interesting than that. Besant and the match factory employees protected and empowered one another in a series of events that led directly to improvements in the factory. Besant's first move was to call for a boycott of Bryant & May matches. People of conscience, she thought, could buy matches from a company that treated its workers better. Besant felt that she had executed her humanitarian duty at that point, and she might have desisted from further action.

However, she discovered, to her horror, that Bryant & May had conducted a bullying search for the employees Besant had interviewed for her editorial 'White Slavery in London'. Besant immediately responded by publishing an open letter to 'Messrs. Bryant and May', in which she called them cowards. In this letter, she hastened to say that, instead of further 'terrorising' their employees, the company directors should sue her for libel. Later, she would point out that what she printed was true, and the Bryants had no case against her. In the same letter, she promised to financially support any girls fired for their testimony. She also started a fundraising campaign to make good on her promise, and announced another meeting to be held to discuss Bryant & May.

Besant's outraged and unequivocal support may have emboldened Bryant & May's employees, but the strike was definitely their idea. The precipitating blow seems to have been the unjust firing of an employee. Bryant & May were trying to drum up a libel case against Besant. To that end, they were combing the factory for signatures on a statement saying that workers were well treated and that Besant was wrong. One unnamed worker, identified as a troublemaker, refused to sign, and she was fired.

The strike began on 5 July and continued through the 6th. Initially, 1,400 women and children stopped working. Bryant & May began negotiations, first offering to rehire the unjustly fired employee. But the strike had gathered momentum, and the workers opened negotiations for more widespread improvements. In particular, they wanted an end to the fines. On 6 July, the entire factory had ceased production due to workers refusing to work.

One hundred matchgirls and match women marched through London to find Annie Besant and ask for her ongoing support. According to Besant's autobiography, these girls immediately noted that they had been asked to sign statements discrediting Besant, and they had refused to do so. 'You had spoke up for us … and we weren't going back on you,'[12] one said.

Most of the individual girls and women who participated in the strike have been effectively lost to history. Current scholarship can produce very few names, even of those who were leading the strike and march. One of the few names we have is that of Sarah Chapman.

Chapman was born in 1862, and lived her entire life in London's east end. She began work at Bryant & May when she was 19 or earlier. (Children often worked at home or part-time before beginning full-time jobs.) As a machinist for the factory, she was one of its most highly paid workers. Her mother and older sister also worked for Bryant & May.

Besant helped the striking matchgirls form a strike committee. Along with Chapman, Mary Naulls, Mary Cummings, Alice Francis, Kate Slater, Mary Driscoll, Jane Wakeling, and Eliza Martin were that committee's first members. Via the strike committee, Chapman was swept up in a world of politics and politicians. She met with members of Parliament and elicited sympathy for the match girls' cause.

Improved conditions at Bryant & May did not occur in a straight line. But the strike and march must have finally impressed upon the

Bryants that they could not simply bully their employees into further silent suffering.

The dreaded fines ended first, taking a considerable stress off the backs of already impoverished workers. The Bryants also reinstated the worker who had been fired for speaking with Besant. The workers successfully negotiated for a dining area away from the phosphorus fumes.[13]

Within half a year of the strike, the match girls and women had formed a union, the largest all-women union in the country at that time. It was called the Union of Women Match Makers. As representative of that union, Chapman participated in the 1888 International Trades Union Congress in London. In 1891, she married a cabinet maker, with whom she had six children. She lived to 83 and was buried in an unmarked grave.

The matchgirl strike became a template for establishing workers' rights. However, reforms did not occur across the board. The strike was not successful in getting Bryant & May to switch over to the less hazardous red phosphorus, even though that company was already importing red phosphorus. It would not be until 1906 that white phosphorus was outlawed by the Bern Convention.

However, Bryant & May's monopoly on match production did take a hit when the Salvation Army opened a rival match factory, using only red phosphorus in production. The same non-profit also campaigned to get retailers to reject white phosphorus matches in favour of those made with worker safety in mind.

And Martha Robertson? What became of her?

Martha was likely a beneficiary of the matchgirl strike. In 1895, when she started working at the factory full-time, the fines had ended. The union was strong, representing workers like Martha in the newspapers and Parliament. She got to eat her lunch in a space separate from the necrosis-inducing phosphorus fumes. She remembered the strike and the subsequent reforms. She told her descendants that the Bryants tried to withhold benefits from their newest employees to minimise their losses.

She married James Lakin and had eight children with him. For most of their marriage, they lived in a basement apartment. After her wedding, she made matchboxes for Bryant & May and pickled onions for a pickle factory. When called on, she was also a midwife and an undertaker. She often had a pot of soup cooking on the stove, made with butcher bones. Her husband served in the First World War and was badly injured. With no veterans' benefits or public assistance of any kind, she nursed him back to life while working sixteen-hour days to feed her children. After his death, she made a second marriage.

She never overcame the poverty into which she was born, but like many other matchstick girls, she had the knack of deflecting pity and a large capacity for enjoying life in the moment. She went on seaside day trips with her Bryant & May co-workers. She was not above accepting a drink at the pub. One of her descendants, who was also a drinking buddy, remembers sitting in a pub with her, when it looked like a fight might break out. At that time, Martha was walking with a cane because she had broken her hip. She said, 'If it kicks off, just prop me up in a corner and I'll take 'em on with my stick.'[14] There spoke a girl who started work at 6 and whose peers instigated perhaps the greatest worker walk-out of all time.

Chapter 8

Reformers and Ragged Schools

It's easy to demonise the Victorian period. Child sex workers, fortunes built on the backs of child labourers, 10-year-olds working twelve-hour days, children in prisons and executed for non-violent infractions, no safety net for orphans or children born to addicts. All these horrors, and more, characterise nineteenth-century England.

So, how did we get from there to here? How did we go from sending children off to work at 10, to the helicopter parents and self-esteem trophies of the twenty-first century?

Justice is a slow machine. Compassion was not invented in the twentieth century or later. Most of the reforms we take for granted today began in the Victorian period also. The horrors of child exploitation did not go unnoticed by the more compassionate members of the middle and upper classes. For every capitalist ruining childhoods to make a profit, there was a reformer who wanted to stop him. When Parliament passed the Employment of Children Act in 1903, members built on more than a hundred years of progress toward recognising that childhood was a unique phase in life, an unprecedented learning opportunity, and that children should not be relegated to full-time manual labour. Somehow, over the decades since Robert Blincoe was apprenticed in Ludlow, children went from being financial assets to being cherished and sheltered innocents.

No one law or movement explains that slow but steady transition. However, compulsory education, child-focused legislation, rising wages, women's empowerment, and smaller families played important parts in ending child labour, child prostitution, child imprisonment, and child hunger, at least in what we have agreed to call the 'Western world'.

Compulsory and Available Education

It is all well and good to forge a law saying that children must be educated, for so many hours a week, for so many years. It is quite another thing to guarantee access to education for children. Beleaguered as they are, no-cost education systems which are available to all children and required of all families were the only solution. The humble truant officer (now reinvented as the education welfare officer) must now be credited with raising the boats of countless poor families. Without someone on the streets, knocking on doors, and counting heads, to enforce the law of compulsory education, MPs passed laws that were more often subverted than obeyed.

The Factory Act of 1802, for instance, should have guaranteed that Robert Blincoe and his fellow factory apprentices received instruction in reading, writing, and maths every day. But Blincoe was lucky he had learned to read at the workhouse; his factory masters had no interest in ensuring even the most basic literacy of their drones.

It is generally agreed that the abject failure of the 1802 Factory Act was due to lack of inspections. But a number of checkpoints had to be neglected to ensure the ongoing ignorance of poor Victorian children. Justices neglected to appoint inspectors, or they neglected to ensure that the visits were on a surprise basis. The inspectors neglected to be above taking bribes. The media, for the most part, neglected to cover issues relating to the poor. Instead of the core academic skills, factory teachers were more likely to dispense a watery cereal of religious clichés aimed at making their students obedient to a corrupt system.

Out of this simmering pot of complacency and corruption arose John Pounds, a man with few advantages himself, who launched the ragged schools. Born in 1766, Pounds intended to follow in his father's footsteps. His father was a sawyer working in the Portsmouth Dockyard, so upon reaching the age of 12, Pounds apprenticed himself to a shipwright. A shipwright's apprenticeship lasts a minimum of four years and involves learning to build and repair ships. Three years into his apprenticeship, Pounds fell into a dry dock. His injuries were permanently disabling, and he was now unable to pursue the career that he had so proudly sought.

It took a long time to recover from his fall, so Pounds redeemed the time by teaching himself to read. His reading agenda, combined with his compassionate temperament, prepared him for a life of thoughtful philanthropy and activism.

Pounds's back injury left him doubled over, unable to stand up straight. He turned to shoe making, and was able to support himself in that trade despite his disability. It transpired that he was not the only member of his family to be disabled. His nephew, Johnnie, was born with in-turned feet, a condition today referred to as 'clubfoot' or, more scientifically, talipes. The treatment of that day consisted of breaking the child's foot bones, rejoining them, and hoping that they healed in a better position. This therapy had a high failure rate and risked making the child even more disabled.

With no medical training except for what he had read, Pounds invented a better treatment. He made shoes that gently pushed his nephew's bones in the direction they needed to grow, in incremental stages. As the feet grew, Pounds would periodically refit his nephew with a new pair of shoes that increased the pressure on the deviant bones, and this process he repeated until his nephew's feet were normal. The current treatment for talipes is basically the same: the feet are placed in a series of casts that modify the shape of the bone. Each cast moves the bones a small way in the right direction. Pounds's invention of an orthopaedic shoe was amazing, but it was not his principal claim on history. That's because Pounds is considered the father of the ragged schools.

The ragged school movement started, unpropitiously, in Pounds's workshop. He had adopted Johnnie by this time, and the boy often brought home his friends. Pounds quickly found that he was able to teach these children to read while cobbling shoes. So that's what he did. He charged nothing, often fed and clothed the children, built a fire for them in winter, had no set hours, and no dress code. A nearly naked child received the same education as anyone else in the workshop that day. For Pounds, it was the only kind and decent thing to do.

It was the start of a revolution.

Pounds's neighbours learned what he was doing, and he accepted contributions of food and clothing for the children, but would take nothing for himself, even though he never earned more than a decent subsistence. According to the testimony of Henry Hawkes who wrote the *Recollections of John Pounds*, the inventor of the ragged schools lived in two rooms, one of them his workshop, the other a private chamber one flight up. The workshop had one tumble-down window, framed with a sill that badly needed repair.[1]

Pounds's following grew, and he took to scouring the poorest streets and alleys of Old Portsmouth for new students. Always, he looked for the most derelict and abandoned children to educate. These were not hard to find. The streets of Victorian England's cities were filled with dirty, loud, hungry urchins, begging and pilfering. These children that caused respectable ladies to pull their skirts back, lest they get soiled – these were John Pounds's students. He lured them back to his classroom by first feeding them a few cooked potatoes. Pounds often taught more than forty students at a time, and he did not neglect practical survival skills. His students learned carpentry, shoe making, and the culinary arts, in addition to reading, writing, and maths. He took them on nature walks and taught them to identify various flora.

He was not the sole engineer of free schooling for the poorest children. But by the time of his death in 1839, Pounds had effectively thrown down a gauntlet, challenging future generations to offer free education to children for whom education had previously been out of reach. Aberdeen Sheriff William Watson grabbed that gauntlet and ran with it.

Watson was something of a wild card, having neither the religious nor the academic training that generally characterised philanthropists of the Victorian era. What Watson did possess was a keen sense that education was the antidote to a life of crime. He was sickened by the number of children, boys usually, who turned up in his court, guilty of some petty theft or misdemeanour. Watson understood that sending these children to prison doomed them to a cycle of crime, prison, crime, prison, punctuated with homelessness and early death. Once he had established a free school, he diverted these boys from prison and sentenced them to receive an education instead. In Watson's Aberdeen school, the crazy notion of required attendance was introduced. Children were also fed three times a day, a powerful incentive to comply with attendance, considering that the average street child was very food insecure and could count on zero meals a day with any consistency.

By 1844, Lord Shaftesbury had formed the Ragged School Union which was instrumental in establishing over 200 such schools over the next eight years. According to some estimates, 300,000 children were educated in ragged schools in the four decades following Pounds's death. Ragged school teachers were typically not paid, and the schools were started up in makeshift accommodation because the movement typically could not afford rent. As such, ragged schools emerged in stables, attics, even railway arches.

By 1846, ragged schools drew the journalistic attention of Charles Dickens who gave them his stamp of approval in a letter to the *Daily Mail*. 'They who are too wretched, ragged, filthy, and forlorn, to enter any other place: who would gain admission into no charity school, and who would be driven from any church door; are invited to come in here, and find some people not depraved, willing to teach them something.'[2]

Dickens's approval of the ragged schools was heavily marked with caveats and cautions. The school he visited was badly underfunded, poorly resourced, unventilated, smelly, and crowded. The girls seemed to be quietly learning on schedule in their segregated section, but the boys' class was subscribed by children who could not even be trusted with a book. All their teaching was oral. It was a necessarily imperfect system, he concluded. These facts may explain why Dickens did not give out the name of the school or anyone associated with it.

The author of *Oliver Twist* quickly recognised, however, that the ragged school he visited was the lesser of two evils. The children in this ragged school were not in prison, and he had been to the prisons.

He had taken visitors to see how children were treated in prisons. Grown men wept to see it, he declared. In his letter, Dickens asked for two things. Visit the prisons, then visit the ragged schools, he urged. However flawed the schools were, they were, at that time, the only real bulwark between badly raised boys and incarceration, the novelist strongly implied. Then he suggested that money used to build new churches be diverted to improve these schools. 'I adjure those excellent persons who aid, munificently, in the building of New Churches to think of these Ragged Schools; to reflect whether some portion of their rich endowments might not be spared for such a purpose,' Dickens tactfully nudged. He did not say, 'maybe it's time to establish some better priorities', but he did urge rich Christians 'to contemplate, calmly, the necessity of beginning at the beginning; to consider for themselves where the Christian Religion most needs and most suggests immediate help.'[3]

The next calendar year, Scottish minister and free thinker Thomas Guthrie published *A Plea for Ragged Schools*, a sort of manifesto which laid out guidelines for this new school system. He called, among other things, for 'cleanliness'.[4] Some historians have painted this as an unwholesome obsession, but Guthrie was certainly not the first or last educator to think that a degree of personal hygiene was desirable in day students.

He also insisted on required attendance and nutrition. Children will not choose school over play voluntarily, Guthrie noted; attendance must be compelled for free schools to work. Ragged students must also be fed, preferably three times a day; many children will happily choose school over the streets when they are guaranteed free meals. These schools, Guthrie went on to say, should not imitate workhouses or residential hospitals, where the children were basically prisoners. The students of ragged schools should study by day and return to the bosom of their families at night. Perhaps Guthrie's most revolutionary guideline was to refrain from corporal punishment. 'Hard words and harder blows are thrown away here. With these, alas! they are too familiar at home, and have learned to be as indifferent to them as the smith's dog to the shower of sparks,' he wrote.[5]

By the beginning of the twentieth century, there had been a sea change in social attitudes toward children. No longer did the average lady, shopping in London, see a threadbare child on the street and think, 'That child should be in prison!' or 'That child should be working in a factory!' No, by 1900, that same lady would likely think, 'That child should be in school.'

Educational philosopher Margaret McMillan put this new thinking into print when she wrote *Early Childhood*. Born in 1860, McMillan became a reformer and advocate for poor children early in life. She was a student, then a colleague of William Thomas Stead. Building on the ragged school revolution, she went on to become the mother of universal school breakfast and lunch.

Early Childhood, published in 1900, does not argue against child labour. It does not have to; by then, the idea of universal and compulsory education was mostly codified in the consciences of right-thinking humans. But in showing how children develop physically, how slowly they develop precise movements, and how voraciously they read and exercise their imaginations, McMillan ennobled childhood. The discoveries she made about what young children were and were not capable of underlie many of the assumptions people make about children today. The point on which she was most insistent, however, was the humble school lunch. Starving children could not learn at an optimal rate, she noted. She conceded that it was the parents' responsibility to feed their children, but also pressed her point that some parents just could not be counted on to do so: 'a certain number of parents in every civilized country ... cannot, or will not, provide sufficient food for their offspring ... thousands of children go breakfastless to school every morning.'[6] McMillan never raised her voice in print, but her gentle and well-reasoned assertions were a driving force in passing the 1906 Provision of School Meals Act.

McMillan's influence on education in the twentieth and twenty-first centuries has probably been underestimated. The Provision of School Meals Act is arguably her most important legacy, but she also advocated for the creation of nursery schools, exposure to the natural world, and learning through play, an idea integral to progressive schools, like the Montessori system, today.

By 1900, it was assumed that the British government not only had a right to intervene in children's welfare, but also a duty to do so. 'By the end of the century, it was coming to be felt that only state action could secure a childhood for all children, and states began to take over from philanthropy the key role in ... saving the child,' writes historian Hugh Cunningham.[7] This governmental duty of child protection was codified in the 1904 Prevention of Cruelty to Children Act which gave the newly formed National Society for the Prevention of Cruelty to Children powers to remove a child from abusive or extremely neglectful parents.

McMillan understood the importance of government intervention to save children, and she helped her readers navigate that transition. In her books, 'the State', always capitalised, figures prominently, though it does not always do enough or behave consistently. McMillan's State always had an indelible role to play, however, in the transition from childhood to adulthood.

The Children's Charter: Decriminalisation of Children

Late Victorians and early-twentieth-century families came to accept that the British government now had a say in how children could be raised. A spate of legislation in the first years of the new century testifies to how thinking about children had changed. Children were no longer the private property of their parents; they could not be starved, beaten, and sent out to work, beg, or steal, with impunity.

The Employment of Children Act in 1903 gave communities broad powers to limit employment to people older than 15. Children hired part-time in factories could not be hired for a second or third job. Children were prohibited from doing dangerous work, especially lifting objects that were too heavy for them. This act had more teeth than earlier legislation because it empowered local authorities to enter factories and other places where children were employed to make sure that the law was being observed. This severely curbed the ability of factories to momentarily cover up infractions prior to a scheduled inspection. The Employment of Children Act did not do away with child labour. By some estimates, over half a million of the United Kingdom's children were working part-time in 1914. But the days of children working twelve-hour days, six days a week, as Robert Blincoe had done, were mostly over.

The Employment of Children Act was quickly followed by the 1908 Children's Charter. This charter, known more formally as the Children Act, repealed or amended forty other parliamentary acts. Like earlier laws, it provided oversight for third-party childcare providers. Anyone caring for a child under 7 and receiving money for doing so had forty-eight hours to inform the local authorities that he or she was doing that job. The new charter prohibited childminders from taking out insurance on the children in their care, thus preventing them from murdering a child for the insurance pay-out.

The Children's Charter expanded parental responsibility and legal liability for the death of their children. No longer could drunk parents roll over and suffocate their children without facing legal consequences. Children under 7 could not be left in a room alone with an unsupervised fire. Children under 16 could not be employed in dangerous jobs. Children under 16 were no longer allowed to smoke. It was illegal to sell cigarettes to children and police were empowered to remove them from a child's possession. Similarly, the charter established guidelines that discouraged children from going into or being taken to brothels and bars.

The greatest and most lasting change made by the Children's Charter was the way child criminals were treated. Children could no longer be executed for any crime, even a violent one. Parents could no longer abandon children who were charged with a crime. Instead, parents were at least partly responsible for their children's infractions. They had to pay any fines incurred by their children's behaviour and take them home.

Perhaps most importantly, children could no longer be sent to adult prisons. Instead, they went to borstals which were the early equivalent of youth detention centres. Borstals had been in existence since the 1800s, and they were named after the first of their kind, a facility in the village of Borstal, Kent. Further legislation, in the form of the Prevention of Crime Act of 1908, laid out how borstals could operate and protected adolescent residents from arbitrary handling.

Borstals were never an optimal method of dealing with child criminals; at present, youth detention centres still have not solved the most critical problems arising from corralling delinquent teens into one facility. In any such facility, bullying can occur, and children have the potential to encourage one another in criminal tendencies. Nevertheless, an important underlying mindset had shifted. The creation of borstals recognised that child criminality was at least partly the responsibility of a failing society, that children did not become morally corrupt as a matter of preference. The Prevention of Crime Act used the word 'reformation' to describe the work of these institutions. The creation of borstals also assumed that education, not punishment, was the key to diverting a child from a life of crime. To that end, borstals were a place of strict discipline, but also a place for learning a trade and receiving at least a basic education. Sentences could not exceed three years without a review. Prison commissioners had the authority to commute a sentence to six months for boys, three months for girls, if the teenager showed promising signs of redemption.

The Children and Young Persons Act of 1933 built on and amended the 1908 act. The new act illustrates just how dramatically attitudes toward children had changed. Where the 1908 act said, in effect, that children were not entirely responsible for their bad behaviour, the new act assumed that child criminals needed protection.

Empowered Women – Living Wages – Smaller Families

In 1859, future suffragette Jessie Boucherett co-founded the Society for Promoting the Employment of Women (SPEW), an organisation that has gone through a number of changes, but still exists under the name Futures for Women. SPEW's original mission was to single women. Victorian women, even those born to wealthy families, lived on the knife edge of financial insecurity because of laws and conventions that kept women from buying property, inheriting property, making money, and saving money. What happened to these women when a brother, father, or husband defaulted on his duty to maintain them? SPEW was invented to solve that problem by opening up paid job opportunities for women. As the Futures for Women website ably notes, employment options for a Victorian lady were far too few. She might find work as a governess, seamstress, or paid companion, but these fields were 'thoroughly oversubscribed and underpaid'.

SPEW did not act alone. Many philanthropists decried the financial vulnerability of women at all levels of society. And many groups were formed and movements launched to help women enter the workforce. Where SPEW excelled was in opening the fields of accountancy, bookkeeping, and office skills to women, providing training and applying political pressure where needed. Through the agency of SPEW, women also cracked open craft guilds that had been occupied solely by men: painting porcelain, watch making, photography, telegraphy, and hair styling.

As the twentieth century progressed, women entered more and more well-paid trades and professions. Not to put too fine a point on it, women who made their own money were less dependent on bad husbands. A working woman could not be bullied or exploited with impunity, and she also had better leverage for protecting her children from being bullied and exploited. In a two-income family, there was much less need for children to work. In a sense, women replaced children as secondary workers while also improving their status in family and community.

The surge of women into the workforce raised the status of women across all sectors. Women who stayed home to cook, clean, and raise children also received a new respect. In North America, around 1890, the lovely word 'homemaker' emerged to describe unpaid, full-time mothers who kept house. This rising status of women went hand in hand with the rising status of children. If motherhood was a cherished vocation, then children must also be worthy of adoration. When children are adored and protected, the people protecting them must be worthy of respect, also.

Contributing to this phenomenon was a change in how families were perceived. 'The Victorian household in which the husband reigned supreme gave way to a more democratic ideal, which scholars refer to as "the companionate family",' writes Lori M. Campbell. The era of the love match had begun, largely because women had alternatives to marrying for financial stability. Young people were not only free to pursue love, they were encouraged to think that marriage would be successful only if the bride and groom had sincerely fallen in love.

In their mostly subsumed work *Revolt of Modern Youth*, Ben Lindsey and Wainwright Evans argue that children are only protected in a marriage characterised by love: 'There is such magic ... in an open and unforbidden love between parents ... That is the only thing that can sanctify the home and protect the children.'[8] In this more democratic marriage, children were highly valued as the natural outcome of their parents' love.

Another factor that independently raised the status of children in the twentieth century was the decline of infant mortality. Science and medical advancements dramatically lowered the chances that a baby would die within a few months of her birth. Once babies were more likely to grow into delightful children, and thence into delightful young adults, parents had greater motivation to invest in them emotionally and financially. Concurrently, women and men were more and more limiting their numbers of children, planning their families. Where there were fewer children, each child was more precious.

While SPEW and other activists were pushing employment opportunities for women, Victorian wage workers generally were pushing for incomes that would support their families. They were supported by Liberal MP Mark Oldroyd. In 1894, Oldroyd gave a lecture, then published a pamphlet in which he coined the term 'living wage'. It put forward the radical notion that full-time workers should not be paid based on the market demand for their products and services. Instead, such a worker should be paid enough to feed and clothe himself and 'those legitimately dependent on him'. Additionally, this should be enough money to live comfortably and discharge 'the duties of citizenship'.[9]

Oldroyd himself was a factory employer, so he was well placed to understand the hardships of the working man. Around the same time that Oldroyd introduced the term 'living wage', other activists and workers were lobbying for a 'minimum wage'. Employers such as Bryant & May were still getting around labour laws by hiring workers on a 'sweating basis'. Parliament eventually responded by enacting the Trade Boards Act of 1909. This act demanded an increase in wages in several historically low-paying sectors, including chain, box, clothes, and lace manufacture. In arguing for this new law, Winston Churchill declared: 'It is a serious national evil that any class of His Majesty's subjects should receive less than a living wage in return for their utmost exertions.'[10]

When it became possible for working men and women to support their children, the pressure for children to go to work was substantially relieved. No examination of the changing status of children can overlook the importance of the minimum wage.

Nor can we overlook the related issue of family planning. The humble condom hit the shelves of London in 1921, decades ahead of oral contraceptives. Women were enjoying greater status in their communities and in their marriages because they had entered the workforce. With condoms added to their arsenal, they started limiting the number of children they had and putting longer intervals between babies. This meant that families could better provide for the children they had. The less is more principle found its finest application in working families. Fewer children meant those children had more resources, more attention, more respect, and better chances of survival.

The Enjoyment of Childhood

Historians generally agree that Charles Dickens was not, himself, a model parent. He loved his children when they were babies, but when they reached the teen years, his enthusiasm for them waned sharply. (This is not an uncommon feature of parenthood.) It didn't help that, when he married Catherine Hogarth, he had a sharper eye on his social advancement than on the couple's compatibility. His growing contempt for his wife did not stop him from having ten children with her, however.

Neither Catherine nor his children could match Dickens's own indefatigable energy. This was, after all, a man who would never retire, never slow down, and who was busily writing *Edwin Drood* the day before his death by stroke. By contrast, Catherine frequently lapsed into postpartum depression. Dickens accused her of lethargy. Of his children, he famously said that he had, 'brought up the largest family ever known with the smallest disposition to do anything for themselves'.[11]

That said, Dickens did his part and more to enshrine childhood as a unique and unrecoverable stage in life. In his novels, he captured childhood's wonder, the ability of children to see ordinary, or even sordid, things as magical. *Oliver Twist* was not his only novel to deify the vulnerability and innocence of children. He created a whole roster of characters who badly needed protection from villainous adults in *Little Nell*, *Great Expectations*, and *David Copperfield*, to name the most famous.

These depictions of childhood did not emerge in isolation. Many Victorians already cherished their children, studiously cultivated them, and protected them even from theoretical exposure to corruption. But this was the exclusive privilege of the upper and middle Victorian classes. And they represented only 25 per cent of the total population. It was inevitable that other Victorian children would feel the brunt of poverty in families that had far more children than their financial resources could support. As wages rose and women had more power both to earn money and scale down their families, more families could reconcile the ideal of the cherished child with their circumstances.

Cunningham writes, 'until the nineteenth century, policies had been drawn up with a concern either for the child's soul or for the future manpower needs of the state. Both of these concerns remained in place in the nineteenth and early twentieth centuries, but they were joined by a new one, a concern to save children for the enjoyment of childhood.'[12]

In the Victorian era, children of working-class or poorer families were expected to earn and contribute to the family income at a very young age. The children of these families did not argue with that expectation, as we have seen from the example of George Elson. By the mid-twentieth century, that expectation had fully shifted. Children were not expected to work. A 12-year-old who had paid employment would be the exception. No one has captured this enormous mindset shift better than Viviana Zelizer who writes that, in fifty years, children transitioned from being financial assets to nurtured and protected investments. 'By the 1930s, lower-class children joined their middle-class counterparts in a new nonproductive world of childhood, a world in which the sanctity and emotional value of a child made child labor taboo.'[13]

By 1950, a family that sent children under 16 into a job outside the home might well be questioned by neighbours or even social workers. Parents were now expected to sacrifice their own welfare, to a substantial extent, so that their children could have a trouble-free existence. Instead of bringing home fabrics for their children to sew or boxes for them to assemble, parents started insuring their own lives to make sure that their children were cared for in their parents' absence. These same parents opened savings and retirement accounts, aiming to be independent in old age and not a burden to their adult children. They established trust funds, or at least college funds, when possible. Failure to give children a stress-free childhood and good options for the future could earn parents a stigma; such a failure could be taken as a sign that they didn't love their children enough. It could be taken as a sign of overall failure to measure up as an adult.

Chapter 9

Miles to Go Before We Sleep

T he conclusion to a book like this must issue a challenge. To pretend that child exploitation and poverty are things of the past would be wholly irresponsible. The problems of child imprisonment, child labour, and child trafficking have dissipated in the United Kingdom. But a round of self-congratulations needs to be postponed until children are better protected globally.

Child Imprisonment: Still a Problem in Countries We Call Civilised

The United Nations Children's Fund (UNICEF) estimates that more than a million children were behind bars as of 2016.[1] It is virtually impossible, however, to get accurate statistics on this issue because many countries do not keep track of their child prisoners. 'Many are held in decrepit, abusive, and demeaning conditions, deprived of education, access to meaningful activities, and regular contact with the outside world,' reports Human Rights Watch.[2] In some parts of the world, children can still be incarcerated for behaviours many Westerners would not identify as crimes: having an abortion, begging, truancy, having consensual sex, drinking alcohol, or running away from home. UNICEF notes that a quantum of such petty crime is still committed under pressure from adults.[3]

Amongst the countries that do track their incarcerated children, the greatest offender is the United States. According to the Annie E. Casey Foundation, 60,000 American children were in juvenile detention facilities in 2011, and an appalling 95,000 were in prisons with adult populations.[4]

Partly, this is a function of the erroneous US belief that some crimes committed by children are too heinous to be addressed with education and treatment for mental health. 'Try him as an adult!' is the cry of families and communities outraged by violence enacted by children. Such outcries often result in teenagers serving time side by side with adult murderers and child molesters. Children and teens in adult prisons are at the mercy of violent offenders. Though torture is not their official sentence, their stay in prison can be torturous. Additionally, the United States, South Africa, and Israel have the distinction of being the only three countries in the world that sentence young people under the age of 18 to a lifetime in prison.

While prisons in these wealthy countries might be cleaner, and their prisoners better fed, than prisons in the poorest countries, efforts to protect children from incarceration need to focus on better solutions for children in developed, tech-savvy nations. Until the most privileged nation states can set an example of civilised behaviour toward their own children, we can hardly preach to the poorest nations on this issue.

Child Labour in the Underworld

According to World Vision, nearly 79 million children were working under hazardous conditions in 2022. The poorest countries have the most children working in dangerous occupations.[5] A 2013 analysis by the data gathering firm Maplecroft showed that Eritrea, Somalia, Democratic Republic of Congo, Myanmar, Sudan, Afghanistan, Pakistan, Zimbabwe, and Yemen were where children most frequently worked. But child labour is by no means a problem exclusive to the third world. The Maplecroft report stated that 100,000 Chinese children were working in factories.[6]

UNICEF declares that children end up in the workforce most often because of financial insecurity at home. The loss of one or both parents, the sudden illness of a caregiver, or the lost job of the primary wage earner usually propel children out of the classroom and into the factory or other workspace.[7]

This is not a problem that is going away. The rates of child labour fell from 2010 to 2016, but the numbers of working children rose steadily in the four years that followed, adding 8.4 million children to legal and illegal work forces. Refugee children and migrants are at high risk of being forced into hazardous labour or being trafficked.

At highest risk, though, are those children living in war-torn countries. Children are routinely pressed into military or quasi-military service against their will and that of their parents. These children are frequently deployed as cooks, porters, messengers, spies, and even frontline armed fighters. 'Between 2005 and 2020, more than 93,000 children were verified as recruited and used by parties to conflict, although the actual number of cases is believed to be much higher,' UNICEF reports.[8] The toll on the psychological health of children in military groups is well documented. Such children are also at high risk of poor nutrition, substance addiction, injury, disability, and, of course, death. As if that were not bad enough, at the end of a military conflict, such children are not always accepted back into their families and communities. Depending on whose side they fought, they may be regarded with suspicion or just told to move on. So little can be done to prevent paramilitary groups from abducting and coercing children into service that UNICEF's efforts focus on providing health care for such children, getting them released from military juntas, reuniting them with their families, or finding other safe spaces for them.

The United Kingdom is unlikely to see a return of 12-year-olds to its factories, but the work that children, globally, do is often even more dangerous. In our time, children are often employed in the drug trade. In Ecuador, children as young as 10 are recruited to sell drugs. The same cartels that lure them into the drug trade then train them as assassins.[9] The Commission on Young Lives, a UK-based non-profit, reported in 2022 that, in England, children as young as 9 were being groomed for work in the drug trade.[10]

Child Trafficking and Prostitution in the Twenty-first Century

Has humanity made progress toward the goal of universal justice? If we look at the issues of child labour and child imprisonment, it is clear that developed nations have made significant strides in the right direction.

Unfortunately, in the arena of child sex exploitation, the march toward enlightenment is much less visible. The same digital tools that make apprehension of criminal behaviour easier also make the entrapment of children easier. Since the Victorian era, there have been so many child sex exploitation scandals that this book will confine its inquiries to the twenty-first century and to activity among children under 14. In 2012, the Greater Manchester Police investigated a sex trafficking ring that involved nineteen men and the exploitation of forty-seven girls, some of them no older than 13. The ring used a 15-year-old girl to recruit others. Police had been alerted to the existence of local trafficking over several years, but each time they deemed the witness unreliable.

In 2014 and 2015, ten Cambridgeshire men were tried and found guilty of raping and trafficking girls as young as 12. The victims were vulnerable in one way or another. Some were members of immigrant families from eastern Europe, some had been taken into care. The traffickers gifted the girls with free meals and cigarettes, then got them drunk and made them listen to pornography for the purpose of exploiting them. Similar rings have been exposed in Banbury, Aylesbury, Bristol, Derby, Halifax, Keighley, Oxford, and Telford.

William Thomas Stead was successful in exposing child trafficking in the 1800s, but the Stead Act, which raised the legal age of consent to 16, has not protected all British teens from sexual exploitation, even in our own time.

In 2016, Member of Parliament Ann Coffey lobbied successfully to erase the term 'child prostitution' from British laws. Her argument was that the term suggested trafficked children were complicit in their own criminalisation. Her campaign was successful in changing the dated rhetoric surrounding the trafficking of children.

But that leaves the hard part: eliminating the trafficking itself. We all want to live in a world where 13-year-olds are not coerced into sex work, where orphans like Robert Blincoe don't become disabled in the process of doing factory work, where children like George Elson don't have to leave home to climb chimneys because there is no safety net. But we don't live in that world. Not entirely. Not yet.

Notes

Introduction: The Worst Poor Law Ever
1. Frost, Ginger S. *Illegitimacy in English Law and Society, 1860–1930.* Manchester: Manchester University Press, 2016, p. 1.
2. Zlotnick, Susan. 'The Law's a bachelor: Oliver Twist, bastardy, and the new poor law.' *Victorian Literature and Culture*, Vol. 34, No. 1 (2006), pp. 131–146, p. 132.

Chapter 1: Boy Interrupted: Dickens's Childhood Twist
1. Chesterton, G. K. *Charles Dickens.* London: Methuen and Company, 1906, p. 25.
2. Ibid., p. 26.
3. Ibid., p. 26.
4. Forster, John. *The Life of Charles Dickens.* London: Chapman and Hall, 1892, p. 23.
5. Chesterton, p. 33.
6. Ibid., p. 37.
7. Marzials, Frank. *Life of Charles Dickens.* London: Walter Scott, 1887, p. 19.

Chapter 2: Roger Blincoe: Workhouse and Factory Survivor
1. Peters, Laura. *Orphan Texts: Victorian Orphans, Culture and Empire.* Manchester: Manchester University Press, 2000, p. 1.
2. Ibid., p. 2.
3. Ibid., p. 7.
4. Waller, Robert. *The Real Oliver Twist.* Cambridge: Icon Press, 2006, p. 99.
5. Ibid., p. 124.
6. Ibid., p. 157.
7. Simmons, James. *Factory Lives: Four Nineteenth-Century Working-Class Autobiographies.* Peterborough, Canada: Broadview Press, 2007, p. 136.
8. Waller, p. 166.
9. Ibid., p. 151.
10. Ibid., p. 150.
11. Ibid., pp. 158–159.
12. Ibid., p. 191.
13. Ibid., pp. 191–192.
14. Ibid., pp. 229–230.

15. Ibid., p. 229.
16. Ibid., p. 232.
17. Ibid., pp. 254–255.
18. Ibid., pp. 325–327.

Chapter 3: The Artful Dodger and Child Criminals
 1. Duckworth, Jeannie. *Fagin's Children*. London: Hambledon, 2002, p. 40.
 2. Ibid., p. 27.
 3. Ibid., p. 36.
 4. Ibid., p. 27.
 5. Ibid., p. 29.
 6. Ibid., p. 51.
 7. Ibid., pp. 51–52.
 8. Ibid., p. 35.
 9. Ibid., p. 35.
10. Knight, Charles. *London: Volumes 3–4*, London: Charles Knight & Co. 1842, p. 267–268.
11. Duckworth, p. 4.
12. Neale, William Beaver. *Juvenile Delinquency in Manchester*. Manchester: Gavin Hamilton, 1840, p. 8.
13. Ibid., p. 9.
14. Ackroyd, Peter. *London, the Biography*. London: Doubleday, 2001, p. 130.
15. Duckworth, p. 42.
16. Ibid., pp. 28–29.
17. Millbank Prison. Hansard, 24 July 1846. api.parliament.uk.
18. Duckworth, p. 49.
19. 'Fatal Case of Military Flogging at Hounslow.' *Edinburgh Medical and Surgical Journal*, 1 October 1846; 66 (169): 395–433.
20. Moore, J.M. 'Reformation, Terror and Scandal: The 1853 Royal Commission into Abuses at Birmingham Prison.' *Midland History* 46, no. 1 (2021), pp. 82–100.
21. Duckworth, p. 76.
22. Ibid., pp. 83–85.
23. Johnson, William Branch. *The English Prison Hulks*. London: C. Johnson, 1957, p. 123.
24. Duckworth, pp. 88–89.
25. Farran, Susan Elizabeth, 'The case of the child convict John Hudson.' Researchgate.net. 2016.

Chapter 4: The Nancies: Child Sex Workers
 1. Duckworth, p. 197.
 2. Dickens, Charles. *The Adventures of Oliver Twist. Also, Pictures From Italy, and American Notes*. Boston: Ticknor and Fields, 1867, p. IX.

3. Ibid., p. 6.
4. Ibid., p. 5.
5. Ibid., p. 5.
6. Duckworth, pp. 189–190.
7. Dickens, *Adventures of Oliver Twist*, p. 226.
8. Rush, Florence. *The Best Kept Secret: Sexual Abuse of Children*. New York: McGraw-Hill Book Company, 1980, p. 64.
9. Dyer, Alfred Stace. *The European Slave Trade in English Girls*. London: Dyer Brothers, 1880, p. 4.
10. Ibid., p. 4.
11. Ibid., p. 5.
12. Ibid., pp. 6–8.
13. Ibid., pp. 9, 12.
14. Ibid., p. 13.
15. Ibid., p. 13.
16. Ibid., p. 13.
17. Stead, William Thomas. *The Armstrong Case*. London, 1885, p. 6.
18. Stephen, James Fitzjames. *Digest of the Criminal Law*. London: MacMillan, 1887, p. 193.
19. Stead, *Maiden Tribute*, p. 11.
20. Ibid., p. 12.
21. Ibid., p. 12.
22. Ibid., p. 13.
23. Ibid., p. 14.
24. Ibid., p. 18.
25. Ibid., p. 18.
26. Rigon, Sara. 'Is my daughter still a virgin?' National Library of Medicine, 2018.
27. Stead, William Thomas. *Maiden Tribute of Modern Babylon*. CreateSpace Independent Publishing Platform, 2015, p. 21.
28. Ibid., p. 21.
29. Ibid., p. 23.
30. Ibid., p. 23.
31. Ibid., p. 39.
32. Ibid., p. 44.
33. Ibid., p. 47.
34. Ibid., p. 49.
35. Ibid., p. 49.
36. Ibid., p. 49–50.
37. Dickens, Charles, 'Appeal to Fallen Women', 1849.
38. Ibid.
39. Ibid.

Chapter 5: From the Brothel to the Baby Farm: Child Abduction

1. Stead, *Maiden Tribute*, p. 59.
2. Ibid., p. 70.
3. Ibid., p. 71.
4. Ibid., p. 71.
5. Ibid., p. 59.
6. Ibid., p. 25.
7. Ibid., p. 25.
8. Ibid., p. 26.
9. Stead, *The Armstrong Case*, p. 2.
10. Stead, *The Armstrong Case*, p. 8.
11. Makepeace, Margaret. 'Eliza Armstrong – still elusive.' British Library. March 2016.
12. Dickens, *Oliver Twist*, 9.
13. Dickens, Charles. *The Universal Edition of the Works of Charles Dickens*, Volume 14, London: Chapman and Hall, p. 142–143.
14. 'The Ogre of Tooting,' *Punch*, Volume 17, 1849, p. 38.
15. Dickens, *Universal Edition*, p. 141.
16. Ibid., p. 145.
17. Ibid., p. 147.
18. Ibid., p. 148.
19. Ibid., p. 148.
20. Greenwood, James. *The Seven Curses of London*. London: Stanley Rivers and Co., 1869, p. 34–35.
21. Moorhead, Joanna. 'The Victorian women forced to give up their babies.' *The Guardian*, 19 September 2015.
22. Ibid.
23. 'Baby farming.' *The Spectator*, 25 June 1870, p. 778.
24. Ibid., p. 779.
25. Ibid., p. 778.
26. Ibid., p. 779.
27. Georgius, D. E. 'Ought baby-farming to be prohibited?' *British Controversialist and Literary Magazine*. 1870, p. 395.
28. Ibid., p. 396.

Chapter 6: George Elson and the Climbing Boys

1. Dickens, *Oliver Twist*, p. 18.
2. Ibid., p. 19.
3. Ibid., p. 19.
4. Cullingford, Benita. *British Chimney Sweeps: Five Centuries of Chimney Sweeping*. Chicago: New Amsterdam Books, 2000, p. 20.
5. Ibid., p. 59.
6. Brackley, Paul. 'Forgotten story of Victorian "chimney boy" George Brewster, whose tragic death saved thousands, to be marked with Fulbourn blue plaque.' *Cambridge Independent*, 7 March 2022.

7. Elson, George. *The Last of the Climbing Boys: An Autobiography, Etc.* London, 1900, p. 57.
8. Ibid., p. 180.
9. Ibid., p. 297.
10. Ibid., pp. 305–306.
11. Ibid., p. 473.
12. Ibid., p. 473.
13. Ibid., p. 513.
14. Ibid., p. 662.
15. Ibid., p. 964.
16. Ibid., p. 1241.
17. Ibid., 1507.
18. Ibid., p. 1557.
19. Ibid., p. 1594.
20. Ibid., pp. 1651–1652.
21. Ibid., p. 1686.
22. Ibid., p. 1686.

Chapter 7: Twists Triumphant: How Matchstick Girls Demanded More

1. Raw, Louise. *Striking a Light: The Bryant and May Matchwomen and Their Place in History.* London: Continuum, 2009, p. 209.
2. Ibid., p. 211.
3. Ibid., p. 211.
4. Ibid., p. 82.
5. Ibid., p. 95.
6. Besant, Annie. 'White Slavery in London.' *The Link.* Issue no. 21 (23 June 1888). Republished at Mernick.org.
7. Ibid.
8. Ibid.
9. Ibid.
10. Ibid.
11. Ibid.
12. Besant, Annie. *Annie Besant, an Autobiography.* London: T. Fisher Unwin. 1908, p. 335.
13. Miller, Joe. 'Bow's brave matchwomen honoured in anniversary celebrations.' BBC, 22 June 2013.
14. Raw, p. 215.

Chapter 8: Reformers and Ragged Schools

1. Hawkes, Henry. *Recollections of John Pounds.* London: Williams and Norgate. 1884, p. 13.
2. Dickens, *Universal Edition*, p. 17.
3. Ibid., p. 21.

4. Guthrie, Thomas. *A Plea for Ragged Schools*. Edinburgh: John Elder, 1847, p. 19.
5. Ibid., p. 19.
6. McMillan, Margaret. *Early Childhood*. London: Swan Sonnenschein & Co. 1900, p. 142.
7. Cunningham, Hugh. *Children and Childhood in Western Society Since 1500*. London: Routledge, 2020, p. 137.
8. Ben Barr Lindsey, Wainwright Evans, *The Revolt of Modern Youth*. New York: Boni & Liveright, 1925, p. 245.
9. Oldroyd, Mark. *A Living Wage*. London: Cardington Street, 1894, p. 7.
10. Trade Boards Bill. 28 April 1909. Api.parliament.uk.
11. Gottlieb, Robert. *Great Expectations: The Sons and Daughters of Charles Dickens*. New York: Farrar, Straus, and Giroux, 2012, p. 17.
12. Cunningham, p. 135.
13. Zelizer, Viviana. *Pricing the Priceless Child*. Princeton: Princeton University Press, 1994, p. 6.

Chapter 9: Miles to Go Before We Sleep
1. 'Justice for children.' United Nations Children's Fund. UNICEF.org.
2. 'Children behind bars.' Human Rights Watch. hrw.org.
3. 'Justice for children.'
4. 'Children behind bars.'
5. 'Child labor: Facts, FAQs, and how to help end it.' World Vision. WorldVision.org.
6. Hunt, Katie. '10 worst countries for child labor.' CNN. 15 October 2013.
7. 'Child labor.'
8. 'Children recruited by armed forces or armed groups.' United Nations Children's Fund. UNICEF.org.
9. 'Drug traffickers groom children as young as ten,' CBS. 16 May 2022.
10. Farrell, Jason. 'Children as young as nine sucked into drug dealing and violence.' Sky.org. 4 November 2022.

Bibliography

Ackroyd, Peter. *London, the Biography*. London: Doubleday, 2001.

'Baby farming.' *The Spectator*, 25 June 1870, pp. 778–779.

Besant, Annie. 'Messrs. Bryant and May.' *The Link*. Issue no. 22 (30 June 1888). Republished at Mernick.org.

Besant, Annie. *Annie Besant, an Autobiography*. London: T. Fisher Unwin. 1908.

Besant, Annie. 'White slavery in London.' *The Link*. Issue no. 21 (23 June 1888). Republished at Mernick.org.

Blincoe, Nicholas. 'Grandad, is that you?' *The Guardian*, Sept. 28, 2005.

Brackley, Paul. 'Forgotten story of Victorian "chimney boy" George Brewster, whose tragic death saved thousands, to be marked with Fulbourn blue plaque.' *Cambridge Independent*, 7 March 2022.

Brown, John. *A Memoir of Robert Blincoe*. Manchester: J. Doherty, 1832.

Bridger, Anne. 'History of Futures for Women.' Futures for Women website.

Campbell, Lori M. *The Twentieth Century Child*. University of Pittsburgh.

Chesterton, G. K. *Charles Dickens*. London: Methuen and Company, 1906.

'Child labour.' United Nations Children's Fund. UNICEF.org.

'Child labor: Facts, FAQs, and how to help end it.' World Vision. WorldVision.org.

'Children recruited by armed forces or armed groups.' United Nations Children's Fund. UNICEF.org.

'Children behind bars.' Human Rights Watch. hrw.org.

Cullingford, Benita. *British Chimney Sweeps: Five Centuries of Chimney Sweeping*. Chicago, New Amsterdam Books, 2000.

Cunningham, Hugh. *Children and Childhood in Western Society Since 1500*. London: Routledge, 2020.

Davin, Anna. *Growing Up Poor: Home, School, and Street in London 1870–1914*. London: Rivers Oram Press, 1996.

Dickens, Charles. *The Adventures of Oliver Twist. Also, Pictures From Italy, and American Notes*. Boston: Ticknor and Fields, 1867.

Dickens, Charles. Author's Preface. *The Adventures of Oliver Twist: Or, The Parish Boy's Progress*. London: Bradbury & Evans, Whitefriars, 1846.

Dickens, Charles. *Appeal to Fallen Women*, 1849.

Dickens, Charles. *The Universal Edition of the Works of Charles Dickens, Volume 14*, London: Chapman and Hall, pp. 139–151.

'Drug traffickers groom children as young as ten.' CBS. 16 May 2022.

Duckworth, Jeannie. *Fagin's Children*. London: Hambledon, 2002.

Dyer, Alfred Stace. *The European Slave Trade in English Girls*. London: Dyer Brothers, 1880.

Elson, George. *The Last of the Climbing Boys: An Autobiography*, Etc. London, 1900.

Farrell, Jason. 'Children as young as nine sucked into drug dealing and violence.' Sky.org. 4 November 2022.

Farran, Susan Elizabeth, 'The case of the child convict John Hudson.' Researchgate.net. 2016.

'Fatal case of military flogging at Hounslow.' *Edinburgh Medical and Surgical Journal*, 1 October 1846; 66 (169): 395–433.

Field, Katherine. 'Murder and misogyny in Victorian London.' National Endowment for the Humanities Seminar, 2012. Published by Studylib.net.

Forster, John. *The Life of Charles Dickens*. London: Chapman and Hall, 1892.

Frost, Ginger S. *Illegitimacy in English Law and Society, 1860–1930*. Manchester: Manchester University Press, 2016,

Georgius, D. E. 'Ought baby-farming to be prohibited?' *British Controversialist and Literary Magazine*. 1870, pp. 395–398.

Gottlieb, Robert. *Great Expectations: The Sons and Daughters of Charles Dickens*. New York: Farrar, Straus, and Giroux, 2012.

Greenwood, James. *The Seven Curses of London*. London: Stanley Rivers and Co., 1869.

Guthrie, Thomas. *A Plea for Ragged Schools*. Edinburgh: John Elder, 1847.

Hawkes, Henry. *Recollections of John Pounds*. London: Williams and Norgate, 1884.

Hardy, Thomas. 'The Ruined Maid.' Poetry Foundation.

Hunt, Katie. '10 worst countries for child labor.' CNN. 15 October 2013.

Johnson, William Branch. *The English Prison Hulks*. London: C. Johnson, 1957.

'Justice for children.' United Nations Children's Fund. UNICEF.org.

Knight, Charles, *London: Volumes 3–4*, London: Charles Knight & Co. 1842.

Ben Barr Lindsey, Wainwright Evans, *The Revolt of Modern Youth*. New York: Boni & Liveright, 1925.

Makepeace, Margaret. 'Eliza Armstrong – still elusive.' British Library, March 2016.

Makepeace, Margaret. 'Whatever happened to Eliza Armstrong?' British Library, 2012.

Marzials, Frank. *Life of Charles Dickens*. London: Walter Scott, 1887.

Mayhew, Henry, Richard Beard, and Henry Tuckniss. *London Labour and the London Poor*. London: Office, 16 Upper Wellington Street, 1851.

McMillan, Margaret. *Early Childhood*. London: Swan Sonnenschein & Co., 1900.

Millbank Prison. Hansard, 24 July 1846. api.parliament.uk.

Miller, Joe. 'Bow's brave matchwomen honoured in anniversary celebrations.' BBC, 22 June 2013.

Moore, J. M. 'Reformation, terror and scandal: the 1853 Royal Commission into abuses at Birmingham prison.' *Midland History* 46, no. 1 (2021): 82–100.

Moorhead, Joanna. 'The Victorian women forced to give up their babies.' *The Guardian*, 19 September 2015.

Neale, William Beaver. *Juvenile Delinquency in Manchester*. Manchester: Gavin Hamilton, 1840.

'The newspaper giant who went down with the *Titanic*.' British Library Press Office.

Boyes, Cathryn. 'Nine transported convicts.' *The New Daily*, 17 October 2021.

'The ogre of Tooting.' *Punch*, Volume 17, 1849, p. 38.

Oldroyd, Mark. *A Living Wage*. London: Cardington Street, 1894.

Peters, Laura. *Orphan Texts: Victorian Orphans, Culture and Empire*. Manchester: Manchester University Press, 2000.

Raw, Louise. *Striking a Light: The Bryant and May Matchwomen and Their Place in History*. London: Continuum, 2009.

Rees, Sian. *The Floating Brothel: The Extraordinary True Story of an Eighteenth-Century Ship and its Cargo of Female Convicts*. United Kingdom: Review, 2002.

Richardson, Ruth. 'Oliver Twist and the Workhouse.' British Library, 15 May 2014.

Rigon, Sara. 'Is my daughter still a virgin?' National Library of Medicine, 2018.

Rush, Florence. *The Best Kept Secret: Sexual Abuse of Children*. New York: McGraw-Hill Book Company, 1980.

Simmons, James. *Factory Lives: Four Nineteenth-Century Working-Class Autobiographies*. Peterborough, Canada: Broadview Press, 2007.

Stead, William Thomas. *The Armstrong Case*. London, 1885.

Stead, William Thomas. *Maiden Tribute of Modern Babylon*. CreateSpace Independent Publishing Platform, 2015.

Stephen, James Fitzjames. *Digest of the Criminal Law*. London: MacMillan, 1887.

Tomalin, Claire. *Charles Dickens: A Life*. New York: Penguin Press, 2011.

Tomalin, Claire. 'The house that Charles built.' *The Guardian*, 20 December 2008.

Trade Boards Bill. 28 April 1909. Api.parliament.uk.

Waller, Robert. *The Real Oliver Twist*. Cambridge: Icon Press, 2006.

Whitemore, Warren. 'Fact and Fiction about Little Sweep Valentine Grey.' *Island Echo*. 14 February 2022.

Zelizer, Viviana. *Pricing the Priceless Child*. Princeton, NJ: Princeton University Press, 1985.

Zlotnick, Susan. 'The law's a bachelor: Oliver Twist, bastardy, and the new poor law.' *Victorian Literature and Culture*, Vol. 34, No. 1 (2006), pp. 131–146.

About the Author

Lynn Marie Hamilton is the author of four biographies: *Gandhi, A Life Inspired*; *The Dalai Lama, A Life Inspired*; *Florence Nightingale, A Life Inspired*; and *Florence Nightingale's Sister: The Lesser-Known Activism of Parthenope Verney*. She lives in Louisville, Kentucky with her husband and their dogs.

Dear Reader,

We hope you have enjoyed this book, but why not share your views on social media? You can also follow our pages to see more about our other products: facebook.com/penandswordbooks or follow us on Twitter @penswordbooks

You can also view our products at www.pen-and-sword.co.uk (UK and ROW) or www.penandswordbooks.com (North America).

To keep up to date with our latest releases and online catalogues, please sign up to our newsletter at: www.pen-and-sword.co.uk/newsletter

If you would like a printed catalogue with our latest books, then please email: enquiries@pen-and-sword.co.uk or telephone: 01226 734555 (UK and ROW) or email: Uspen-and-sword@casematepublishers.com or telephone: (610) 853-9131 (North America).

We respect your privacy and we will only use personal information to send you information about our products.

Thank you!